JUMPING THE FENCE

❧

To my late cousin Andre Lebert on his 100th birthday

ISBN 13: 978-1-4621-1383-5

Published by Plain Sight Publishing, an imprint of Cedar Fort, Inc.
2373 W. 700 S., Springville, UT 84663
Distributed by Cedar Fort, Inc., www.cedarfort.com

LIBRARY OF CONGRESS CATALOGING-IN-PUBLICATION DATA

Gilmer, Maureen, author.
Jumping the fence : a legacy of race in 150 years of family secrets / by Maureen Esnard Gilmer.
    pages cm
History of a prominent racially mixed family in New Orleans consisting of the related Esnard and Dejan families.
ISBN 978-1-4621-1383-5
1. Racially mixed families--Louisiana--New Orleans--Genealogy. 2. New Orleans (La.)--Genealogy.
3. New Orleans (La.)--History--19th century. 4. New Orleans (La.)--History--20th century. I. Title.

F379.N553G55 2014
929.20973--dc23

                                 2013033432

Cover design by Angela D. Baxter
Cover design © 2014 by Lyle Mortimer
Edited and typeset by Whitney Lindsley

Printed in the United States of America

10 9 8 7 6 5 4 3 2 1

Printed on acid-free paper

A LEGACY OF RACE
IN 150 YEARS OF FAMILY SECRETS

MAUREEN ESNARD GILMER

PLAIN SIGHT PUBLISHING
AN IMPRINT OF CEDAR FORT, INC.
SPRINGVILLE, UTAH

CONTENTS

———— ⚜ ————

ACKNOWLEDGMENTS

THIS PORTRAIT OF THE ESNARD-DEJAN FAMILY COULD not have been created without the support of the following people: My husband, Jim Gilmer, who put up with my obsession for twenty long years; my literary agent, Jeanne Fredericks, who believed in this story; my editor Haley Miller for her insight and all at Cedar Fort, Inc., for publishing this book; librarian Florence Jumonville, PhD, of the Earl K. Long Library at University of New Orleans, and her heroics in obtaining documents in the wake of Hurricane Katrina; Cathleen Fitzgerald, New Orleans archival expert whose incredible acts of genealogical kindness revealed so much of the story.

And all of those friends and family who generously shared their resources and support for all these long years.

Thank you one and all.

---⚜---

FOREWORD

AUREEN GILMER AND I ARE SECOND COUSINS, BUT our families were not close. So when I met her for the first time, it was relatively late in life; we got together to share some photographs of our great-great-uncle Adrien Esnard, a Catholic priest, a missionary to the Belgian Congo, and by all accounts an extraordinary man. What no one in the last two generations of Esnards seemed to know, however, was that Adrien was seen by people in his era as "colored," despite the fact that his brothers and sisters, from the same parents, were "white."

It was Maureen's unstoppable curiosity and determined research into the life of Adrien and his family that unearthed this fact and the larger story of the Esnards of nineteenth-century New Orleans—a mixed-race family that later moved into the ranks of the "white" world.

The story that Maureen found in the historical records casts a personal and compelling light on a little-known aspect of race in America: the struggles of people of mixed races. The stories of mixed-race people tend to get lost in the intense polarization that so often takes place around race. But some mixed-race families had unique experiences rarely accounted for in our general sense of racial history.

New Orleans was perhaps the one place in America that, thanks to its French and Spanish roots, had a nuanced view of race. It was one of the few places that had an accepted mixed-race community, and it was the only place in the South where "free people of color" could own property and enjoy the fruits of their own enterprise. Yet the failure of Reconstruction and the resurgence of white supremacy embodied in Jim Crow laws made life more and more difficult for both dark- and light-skinned people in New Orleans.

Maureen provides the reader a view of this extraordinary set of circumstances that surrounded mixed-race families. She has done careful research to provide a historical frame for the family members and uses her empathy and imagination to create dialogue consistent with the characters and the facts that marked their lives. I think it is a fascinating story at so many levels, from its broad historical implications to its very intimate and personal dynamics between husbands and wives, and parents and children.

Readers will find this to be a unique and original book. Many mixed-race families like ours have tried their best to forget their origins. This intentional forgetting took these stories not just out of family lore but also out of our general sense of our country's history. I am fairly certain my own father did not know the full story of his father, Rene, nor of Rene's family. And like so many things, our ignorance of our family's history prevented a deeper understanding of the choices they made in the face of segregation and what kind of people they became as a result. My own family's experience makes so much more sense to me now. I hope this book helps others to make more sense of theirs.

MICHAEL ESNARD, PhD
Idyllwild, California

———— ⚜ ————

THEY SAY CHILDREN OF TODAY HAVE LOST THEIR LINKS to the past, and I am afraid with my passing this story of our family may disappear. Unless I tell you about them, the ones who came before us, knowledge of them will be lost once again. You see, it was gone when I began my search. For twenty years I have sought to find them again so that you might come to recognize your legacy as I have. And perhaps then you won't seek to hide it as others have done before, because this is our pride, our accomplishment, and we live as we do today because of them.

⚜

PROLOGUE:
THE OBSESSION IS BORN

HIRTY YEARS AGO, MY HUSBAND, JIM, AND I JOINED MY
father to go to my grandmother Benita Esnard's house on Rimpau
Street in Los Angeles after she died. We were picking up the washing
machine and some other items for my new house. In the attic I found a large
box of family photos, which I studied all the way home in the car. Among
them was a large metal button the size of a dessert plate, like the ones used
during political elections. On it was an odd picture of a bearded Catholic
priest in a white cassock, a cross pinned to his chest. The man's hair was
dense and kinky but combed down into
a flat top. His eyes were deep and dark
beneath bushy brows that are the hall-
mark of Esnard family men.

As he drove, my father would explain
that the man was his great-uncle Adrien,
a priest who died in the Belgian Congo a
long time ago. Dad was a small boy when
Adrien came back to visit his family on
Raymond Street in Los Angeles, and he
remembered the priest well. He would
tell us that Adrien was the source of those
leopard pelts in our home when I was a
child.

Somehow that button picture spoke
to me. I carried it around my ramblings
across California for a long time. It was

This photo of Adrien Benjamin Esnard,
CICM, was taken upon his ordination to
a missionary order. The photo is the first
step of a thousand-mile journey to discover
why he spent his life in the Belgian Congo.

1

not until after I became a writer that I grew curious about this fellow and how he ended up in deep dark Africa. After all, he was in Congo, not civilized Cape Town or Kenya, but Conrad's heart of darkness in the center of that continent. And what made him so different from his sister, my Aunt Florentine, that he would walk away from a prosperous moneyed family? Then I began to wonder what made him leave home at all, because his many siblings, according to Dad, all stayed close to their parents.

Nobody seemed to have any answers. The man's story was a complete mystery except that he had come from New Orleans like the rest of Dad's family. I then succumbed to the curiosity; perhaps there was some magical voice from the past that insisted I inquire about this odd man's strange life. I decided to write one of our distant relatives, an old Frenchman interested in genealogy, Andre Lebert in Sur Seine, just outside Paris.

That first letter to Andre began two decades of research that revealed the story that follows, uncovered in bits and pieces from Europe, Africa, and Louisiana. I worked my way backward to uncover every member of the family and his or her role in why Adrien ended up in Africa. Some of the materials I found came from public records, other parts of it from family letters and, even more surprising, from books and scholarly journals that cite the Esnards specifically. It was amazing to find them detailed in probate inventories, real estate transfers, chess matches, government offices, university archives, and the courts.

Each person that emerged became a piece of the large puzzle that would, in time, create the big picture of this family. The magnitude of its whole would soon eclipse the story of Adrien while explaining his life and choices in so many ways.

In time the family became as real to me as my living relatives. Sometimes their own words written in Victorian hand as well as court testimony gave me special insight into their personal challenges and role in this story. I became the only one who knew all of them by name, their relationships, and, sometimes through rare photos, their appearance. All, particularly Adrien, came alive again to become a real part of my daily life.

After the research wrapped up, I began to write this story. Immediately I realized I could not do them justice without personalizing them for my readers. I just imagined how they would be under the family, social, and religious structure of their day in New Orleans. And as this complex history of a difficult time of racial struggle came tumbling out, they spoke to me, helping my mind to connect the dots of documented historical fact with the realities of the human condition. This familiarity made it quite natural to create fictionalized scenarios for the early Esnards to illustrate the tragedy and struggle of interracial marriage under slavery, and later again during Jim Crow. Though all characters may not be wholly truthful, they do help readers understand the hidden anguish and fear that plagued free people of color.

This dramatization does not, however, cloud the massive amount of factual data expressed in this story. It remains a true history of a family validated by world events and documented by my extensive files. Through the files these people can be studied further for their role in the civil rights movement of the nineteenth century. These files are unique because colored families in New Orleans lived and conducted business under the cloak of secrecy. The Esnards are among the few who generated enough of their own history to support significant revelations nearly two hundred years later. This would be enough to contribute a fresh and little-known view of a tiny enclave sequestered in the heart of early America and its struggle for racial equality.

ENARD/ESNARD FAMILY TREE

New Orleans & Los Angeles

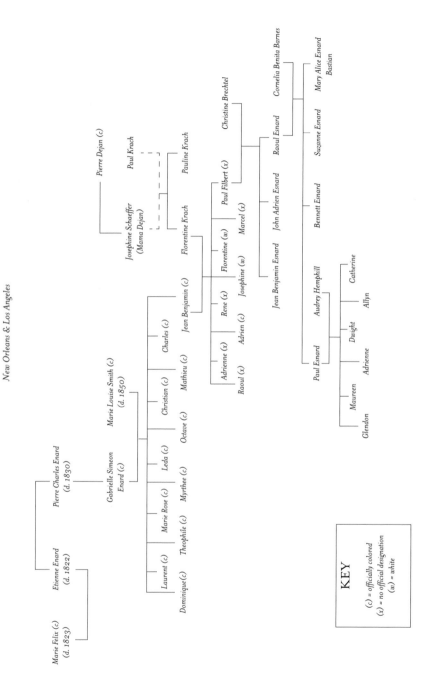

KEY

(c) = officially colored
(x) = no official designation
(w) = white

PART I

LOUISIANA

NEW ORLEANS, 1879

I T WAS HURRICANE SEASON WHEN THE SKIES LAY COAL
black over the rooftops of the French Quarter. Rain threatened to cool
the day, but it only descended like a wet blanket upon the soggy city; air
was as stagnant as a pond, the darkness causing mosquitoes to rise from the
bayous well before evening. Florentine Esnard lay on the brass bed, her belly
swollen beneath the damp sheet, her face pink with the heat of her labor.

This is a rare portrait of Josephine Schaef-fer-Krach-Dejan, affectionately known as Mama Dejan, who became the matriarch of the family in nineteenth-century New Orleans. She left her daughters, Florentine and Pauline Krach, in Alsace Lorraine, France, when she immigrated to Louisiana well before the Civil War to search for her missing husband, Paul Krach.

She waited patiently for her mother, Jose-phine, fondly dubbed Mama Dejan, to return with fresh water to cool her per-spiring brow.

"Just a breath, God. Just a breath of breeze," Florentine prayed through dry lips, but her petitions left the sheer cur-tains hanging heavy and listless in the still air. Through the lace she could see past the cast-iron balcony to the steeple of St. Louis Cathedral that rose far above the rooftops. She had counted the hours of her labor by the ringing of the bells, which marked the sequential passing of every day.

To date, Florentine's brood of chil-dren included Raoul, Paul Filbert, Adrienne, their only daughter, and the youngest boy, Rene. When labor began, she sent each one to a neighbor's house. Their neighborhood butted up to the east border of the old French Quarter boundary of Esplanade Avenue. The Esnards lived in apartments behind the corner store where Mama Dejan sold furniture.

The pain made Florentine feel so alone she missed her sister Pauline more than ever. Though they came from France together about eight years before, Pauline only lived with her for a short time in the new city, choosing to return to France after the first year. Florentine would never forget twelve months of continuous complaints about the climate, the mud, and the strange way of life in what she called "this swamp of a city." Pauline longed for the green countryside of Alsace, where the girls had been raised by their mother's relatives, the Schaeffer family. And that boy, Emil Biche, kept writing letters to Pauline, begging her to return. After each one arrived, the girl became impossible to live with, and when she finally sailed for Europe, Florentine was almost glad to see her leave.

As Florentine rested between contractions, she wondered if her father had died alone or if someone was with him in his final hours. She prayed that if no one was there, then hopefully the Virgin had comforted him, for death by yellow fever was protracted and painful.

Before the Civil War, Josephine Schaeffer-Krach was dubbed Mama Dejan just after she married Pierre Dejan. When the girls finally sailed toward America after the war, they were adult women. Between bouts of seasickness, Florentine and Pauline argued. They discussed their mother's decision to leave them behind. They opined about this now strange woman who bore them and often fought over whether or not she tried to find their father before becoming involved with the new man. Florentine already resented him just because he had taken their father's place in their world. She doubted the love of any mother who would leave her daughters to sail thousands of miles to a city she'd never seen, to find a man who had vanished without a trace.

"She should have looked harder for Papa," Pauline whined as she sipped lukewarm sweet tea after the sea had calmed enough to come up on deck. There the rigging slapped against the main mast with creaking from its monster yard arm.

"We don't know how hard she searched for him, so don't assume she didn't," Florentine snapped, growing tired of Pauline's continuous complaining. "She'd go to the church, I'm sure. They would know. Papa was a good Catholic and never missed Mass."

"He never sent a single letter."

"You don't know that for sure. We just didn't receive one, that's all. It doesn't prove he didn't write. Don't be so quick to criticize Mama. You don't even remember her, do you?"

Pauline looked away and mumbled, "I didn't want to come. It wasn't fair to make me leave Emil."

"She wants us to live with her now that she has a new husband and he's found a house for us."

"I don't want to live with the new man."

"You won't have to, Pauline. Don't be so quick to judge them. It's generous enough to provide us with lodging, but I want you to remember something. We're the only ones to carry on Papa's name. Stop thinking about yourself and be considerate of his memory. How would you feel if I didn't approve of Emil?"

"I don't care if you like Emil or not."

Florentine struggled to hold back her temper, but deep inside she agreed with her sister's dissatisfaction, reserving her own resentments for when they reunited with their mother and all questions could be answered. "You heard me ask Mrs. Schaeffer why our mother didn't bring us with her. All she said was 'Sometimes a woman must follow her husband at all cost.'"

"At the cost of her children."

"She didn't give us up forever; it was just until she could find a place for us to live."

Pauline still wasn't satisfied. "So it took her eight years to find a home?"

When Florentine opened her eyes after the latest contraction, Mama Dejan stood over the washbasin, dampening a cloth with a freshly drawn pitcher of cold water. She bore her typical dour face beneath a mountain of white hair piled tightly atop her head. She wrung out the muslin and then paused to gaze out the window that opened onto the street. Florentine knew she was listening for the sound of Doctor Degas's buggy horse clip-clopping down the street. Outside, the neighborhood was still and quiet; everyone was driven indoors by the oppressive humidity of a summer afternoon.

It was another six hours before the child was born. Florentine was exhausted and soaked, her bedclothes wet from the effort to push the little boy into the world. He would be Adrien Benjamin, she decided, named for her sister's oldest son combined with the name of her child's father, Jean Benjamin. As she nursed him, Florentine's brow knitted as her fingers explored the child's hair, tightly curled into fine patches on his slightly dusky head. She picked up a slip of paper from the nightstand for what must have been the tenth time. It was a copy of the certificate of home birth filled out by the doctor, which was required by law. It was written in his scholarly hand, the ink barely dry. Her eyes went to the same line over and over to find something she dreaded, something she could not change. It was the part where the racial designation of the newborn would be filled in as black, white, or colored. This boy was the first and only one of Florentine's children to be filled in with a C, which designated him colored.

Doctor Degas could not come to the house that day. Another physician, an Irish immigrant from the Channel, arrived, explaining that Doctor Degas had come down with heat prostration. That morning, Doctor Degas had driven out to a plantation to treat colored workers mangled in a cane crusher. He was always called for these matters because he was high yellow with only a few drops of Negro blood. Everyone knew white physicians would not treat black field hands, and even if they wished to, it was not allowed under the new laws in 1879.

Though this substitute physician was quite competent in delivering a child, he didn't know the Esnards or Mama Dejan and barely spoke French at all. He had not lived in New Orleans long enough to know the Esnards were a colored family, quite well-known in the oldest quarter of the city. This man could not be counted on in certain private matters as Degas was. This Irishman did not understand the long-term effects of his visual evaluation of the child and the inevitable conclusion that the infant was indeed not white nor all black. The child would, from that day forward, dwell in that hazy middle ground, stigmatized by a birth record that designated Adrien Benjamin Esnard unquestionably in the "colored" class.

Mama Dejan dreaded Jean Benjamin's return because she would be the one to break the news. Doctor Degas had worked with him in the birth of Raoul, Paul Filbert, Rene, and Adrienne. For these previous births, the racial designations were all W or left blank. The city bureaucrats could overlook an omission if the physician had simply failed to complete that part of the form. But had Doctor Degas designated a colored child as white, his actions would have been considered perjury and a lie. It would damn him in the eyes of the now-heavily white government.

Florentine and her husband knew all too well that this Esnard boy born in the summer of 1879 was now officially colored and, as a result, it damned them all as well.

JEAN BENJAMIN ESNARD

French Quarter, 1879

I T HAD BEEN ONE OF THE MOST CHALLENGING CHESS games he had ever played with Paul Morphy, and that win on the day of Adrien's birth had raised Jean into the elite of Bourbon Street masters. It was just a gentlemanly game and not a competition, for by then Morphy had ceased public chess demonstrations altogether. That was how Jean liked it, modest and personal. He knew that there was a price to pay for notoriety, and he preferred to keep a low profile by limiting his interests to a quiet local life.

It was so hot that day they played out on the *banquette*, sitting around a small table on terribly uncomfortable chairs that barely held Jean's rather

generous bulk. The stub of a fat cigar protruded from beneath his large bristly mustache, scattered ashes dotting his dark silk vest. Jean's forehead was beaded with drops that had made his oiled black hair seem even thicker. Large dark eyes looked out beneath long curved lashes, *bedroom eyes* they would have been called, hooded and unfathomable. This depth is what made Jean Benjamin such a formidable opponent, whether it was at chess, cards, or real estate. He was difficult to read, offering a blank mask or a haughty laugh that revealed only a white, perfectly square set of teeth. There was little to reveal his strategy in life, business, or games.

Jean Benjamin Esnard was born in the French Quarter to an old Creole family of eleven children. He would marry white French immigrant Florentine Krach, the eldest daughter of Josephine Schaeffer-Krach-Dejan.

The sun was low in the western sky and shadows stretched long across the streets when the game finally ended. Morphy counted bills into Jean's large, meaty palm while bystanders also satisfied their own bets on the game. Jean chewed the stub of the same cold cigar, a smile turned up at the edge of his lips into that evil grin that women found irresistible. Just as the last bill was counted, he remembered the messenger boy had come to tell him the baby was on the way. When had that been? Hours ago, surely; the chess game seemed to last forever. Jean suddenly stood up, grasping the silver head of his walking stick as he pocketed the large wad of cash into his baggy, striped trousers. He bid his friends good-

Florentine Krach-Esnard, the eldest daughter of Mama Dejan, married Jean Benjamin Esnard in a civil ceremony during the brief period of legal interracial marriage between Reconstruction and the rise of a Jim Crow law that once again banned such marriages.

bye, then hustled down the banquette through the warren of narrow muddy streets.

After the third child was born, Jean Benjamin lost that flighty feeling of nervousness, realizing his wife, Florentine, was perfectly built for childbearing. Her deliveries were always uneventful. Now that the births had become more routine, he quickly tired of waiting through the long labor at home and often sought out a nearby game. But this time, Jean planned to be back in time to ensure Doctor Degas filled out the certificate just so; a lot depended on how it was done. Lucky for them, Mama Dejan owned the building where Doctor Degas rented his office space. She kept the monthly fee low enough to encourage his loyalty, thereby guaranteeing the right omission on each grandchild's birth record.

Jean knew all too well how important this was. He was born with the C, though he was easily light enough to pass. With such a record, however, anyone could verify his charade. Long ago he had gone to great lengths to make sure his record became lost. He destroyed the copy held by his father, Simeon, along with the more difficult task of doing away with its twin on file at the recorder's office. This was not easy, for it cost a good deal to bribe the night watchman to find the right certificate and remove it from the files. The old man was paid well, for he risked his life to accomplish such a task.

Although this may have helped keep the truth of Jean's ancestry a

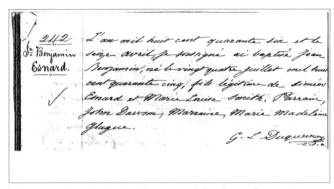

The New Orleans birth index does not include a listing for Jean Benjamin Esnard, while every one of his siblings are accounted for. Only this Catholic baptism record written in French remains to designate Simeon Enard and Marie Louise Smith as his parents.

secret, a true solution was far more complex than that. When he was born over thirty years before, everyone knew his mother, Marie Louise, had no last name. Jean had heard rumors that she had once been a slave but never dared ask whether it was true. Upon the birth of each of Simeon Enard and Marie Louise's colored children, the recorder designated her maiden name as Smith, the most common American name at the time. It seemed most logical choice since the region had so recently become a part of the United States in the Louisiana Purchase.

The moment Jean entered the house he heard the child cry. Mama Dejan came down the hall, wiping her hands on her apron soiled with blood and wet patches. Jean saw something in Mama Dejan's eyes and momentarily thought there had been a problem in childbirth. But Mama held up her hand. "They're both alive," she announced. "It's another boy."

"Then why aren't you smiling? Was I too late coming home?" Jean felt the tickle of fear in the pit of his stomach.

Mama Dejan came closer as Jean closed the front door. Then in the dimly-lit foyer she whispered, "Doctor Degas was ill, Jean. His office sent another doctor instead."

Jean's face fell, for he knew what it meant. Mama Dejan silently retrieved a slip of folded paper from a pocket beneath her soiled apron and handed it to Jean. He studied the birth record closely, then sighed deeply. "At least it's not stating he's black," he said flatly.

"No, but he will be a man of color, and there's no way to get around it now."

In 1879, a birth record with *B* would designate the boy as Negro and no different from a former slave. Jean knew "black" was the lowest caste of New Orleans, and anyone with such a record would find it damned difficult to become educated or obtain employment above that of a mere laborer or domestic. Jean's only consolation was knowing that the infant could be grouped with the rest of his own ten siblings who were all born colored.

That night they allowed the children to come home to meet their newest brother. Paul Filbert, the second son, reached out to touch tight rings of light downy baby hair that spotted the infant's crown. Jean flinched as his son did so, knowing it may prove to be nappy when it finally grew out. His full lips moved slightly beneath the curtain of the mustache, praying that the baby's hair would straighten as it matured just like his own. After a short time, Mama Dejan returned to put the children to bed before she went home to her husband, Pierre.

Later that evening, Jean sat on the bed while his wife held their infant sleeping quietly.

"Can you change it?" Florentine asked, already knowing the answer to her question.

"This isn't the same city anymore. You know that, my dear," Jean Benjamin said. "The way things are for our people now, it's not worth the risk of trying to bribe officials to change it as I did before. If I try now and they discover me, I would certainly be prosecuted. A fair trial would be impossible."

"It's a lynching that worries me most. Adrien's future will be difficult, but if they come after you, we all suffer."

Jean's eyes filled as he glanced at his fourth son. In the faint light of oil lamps, the infant's complexion appeared even darker. Jean's fingers fumbled with an unlit cigar because smoking was banned in the house. "Florentine, you're a strong woman. Few are willing to marry a colored man like me."

"Few see you that way now."

"That is how our people feel, but the white men in the statehouse are the ones who matter most. They know me all too well. Now it's a double burden for you. You'll have to cope with both me and Adrien."

Jean leaned over to pick up the little one. "How can anyone think this beautiful child is anything but perfect?" He continued peering at the tiny pinched face.

"When I agreed to marry you, Jean, I understood that there would be difficulties. But God told me that if my mother could marry a colored man and be happy, then I could too."

"But there's a big difference. Your mother didn't have children with Pierre. You and I, we can bear it, but it's the little ones I worry about. Morphy says the Democrats have just one aim now, to prevent us from living freely as we did before the war. It's fortunate that we are already married because soon they will deny us even that."

It had not always been so difficult to be colored in New Orleans. When Jean Benjamin was born before the Civil War, the city was a different place. His mother, Marie Louise died shortly after giving birth to twins when he was a child, leaving a large number of siblings—ten of them—to care for each other. Their father, Simeon, tried his best to earn enough money to survive and pay for a series of black nurse maids to care for the children. The Esnards had the run of those streets in the Quarter, which became a large and quite familiar backyard with its narrow alleys and extended families.

The Esnards were indeed a mixed bag, especially by New Orleans standards. Jean's mother, Marie Louise, was a beauty. She had light skin, the color of a beignet, golden and clear. Her eyes were amber beneath a mane of thick, curly hair. Marie had no birth certificate like those born in bondage, but once in New Orleans and freed by Simeon, she lived without fear so long as she remained within the city. Simeon made her one of the *gens de coleur libre*, the free people of color who filled their Marigny neighborhood and were rapidly flooding into Tremé.

Before the war, the Esnards were like all other free colored families—they could not travel outside the city limits without risk of being arrested as runaway slaves. After the war, they won great new freedoms for a while. By the time Adrien was born, the extended family of Esnards still living in the Quarter had grown afraid again. Jean had joined the Union Army and later held office during Reconstruction, making him a target. Their family's ancestry was well known to the community no matter what a doctor wrote on the birth record.

Mama Dejan and Florentine were the only whites in the family, documented as French immigrants. The rest of the family were colored no matter how light or dark their skin or how fine or coarse their features. In 1874, when Jean and Florentine married, white women did not consort with colored men, much less marry them. It was still legal at the time, but with politics becoming more segregated every day, there was no telling how long that would last.

With such an unusual relationship, Florentine and Jean lived each day with growing fear that the marriage would doom them and worse, deem their children illegitimate. They had purposefully married in a civil court rather than the church to ensure that the city and the state recognized and recorded their union as legal. But even so, laws could change; it was happening every day. Their state representatives rapidly became more uniformly Southern Democrats, the party of white former Confederates with an ax to grind.

Laws passed since the end of Reconstruction incrementally revoked the civil rights they had all once celebrated. The unwritten laws were even worse—a code of behavior that strictly controlled how colored men or women should behave in the presence of white citizens automatically deemed their superiors. It was concluded that anyone who was born with a single drop of Negro blood would be doomed to the colored class. How that was determined was equally illogical. The Esnards were like so many other free colored families in the neighborhood except that they had stepped over a line few dared to cross. The love of white women for their colored husbands made every day of their life an act of civil and social disobedience.

In the darkness of their bedroom, Jean held Florentine and the baby close as his wife cried, not only for the future of the new little boy, but also for their own hopes and dreams of living without fear. The once-promising years of Reconstruction had faded, and now their world was changing once again. The comfortable cocoon of the Quarter was no longer a safe place for their kind, nor would it ever become the same bastion of freedom in the depths of a hostile land as it was before the war.

As they dressed for bed, Florentine laid Adrien in the small cradle tucked into the corner of their bedroom. She donned a fresh nightgown and watched Jean puff the last of his cigar out on the balcony. "There are too many Esnards in this city to keep secrets any longer," he said without turning back toward her.

"That's true, Jean. We are the only Esnard family in the Quarter, and you are so well known from the legislature."

"My concern is that your mother's store and investments will be of interest to those men. They lost everything in the war and they want it back. They'll try to take her fortune, which is your inheritance, my dear Florentine. I fear they will stop at nothing to get it."

PART II

EUROPE

⚜

JOSEPHINE SCHAEFFER

A.K.A. MAMA DEJAN

Alsace Lorraine, France, 1830

L ITTLE JOSEPHINE SCHAEFFER DREAMED OF THE GUIL-
lotine. That relic of the revolution stood in the village of Dinsheim, not
far from their little farm. She grew up hearing stories about the French
Revolution at a time when struggling with famine and poverty made the bare
necessities of life so difficult to obtain. It was the wreckage of Louis XVI,
who waged his frivolous wars to bankrupt the country while he and Marie
Antoinette continued to lavishly entertain themselves.

Josephine was a child of the Alsace Lorraine region of France, a land of
beautiful and productive farms and that abutted the border with Germany.
But farmlands suffered from the result of so many young men conscripted
into the army. That, combined with many years of inclement weather, weakened crops for consecutive poor harvests. Sky-high prices prohibitively
placed on the basics of life only drove peasants to rise up and dispense with
the monarchy.

These tales included mass executions of anyone considered in league
with the royals. For the unlucky, simply being accused was enough to die at
the hands of Madame Guillotine. She was so hungry for lives, they used to
say, that the execution machine marched through little girls' nightmares like
a monster.

By the time Josephine was born, the revolution was long past. The new
democracy was more peaceful, though the economy was still a challenge for
small merchants and farmers struggling to get by. Naturally every mouth
to feed was a burden, so when Josephine was just a teen, her mother began
seeking out a suitable husband for her, preferably a young man who owned
his land rather than renting it as the Schaeffers did.

Paul Krach was a rural farmer of Obernai, a winemaking center of Alsace that had been traded back and forth between France and Germany for centuries. At the time it was French, therefore the demands of Napoleon's empire-building made it difficult to earn good money on farmland due to the perpetual political upheaval. Soldiers were often stationed in this abundant region, and the Krach farm was among many selected to supply the soldiers with food. The government was unwilling to compensate the Krachs other than with a paper promise of repayment sometime in the distant future.

They couldn't escape the yoke of government nor could they save money. It was quite natural for Paul to become involved in certain circles that had hoped for universal suffrage—a wider set of civil rights for the lower classes— for peasant farmers in particular. This led him further afield as he traveled about the countryside speaking with other farmers who lived in remote locations where there was little access to the news. He sought to galvanize them into a collective political force in support of his cause.

It was on one of these visits to Dinsheim that Paul met Josephine after he spoke to a growing crowd in the park. It was market day and other dissatisfied farmers had streamed in from every direction. Josephine sat on a bench well beyond the crowd listening to the young man speak. He was stocky and had dark hair and eyes, his muscled frame built upon years behind the plough. She sensed he was a man of conviction, judging by his words that spoke for all the illiterate farmers in the region.

After the crowd dissipated, Josephine had just begun the slow walk back to find her parents when a tap on the shoulder proved to be that stocky young man, his eyes twinkling as he bowed slightly. Then he straightened and held out his hand. "Will you join me for a cup of coffee or tea, mademoiselle?"

"We've never been introduced."

"I'm Paul Krach, of Obernai. My farm is fifty acres of bottomland along the river. It's good soil and if the soldiers would cease stealing my livestock, I might someday become a rich man."

"So that's why you're speaking out?"

"I work too hard to give it all away without compensation. And where do you live, my dear?"

"Just out of town beyond the forest in Alsace. My mother says we have the same difficulties, but she doesn't think we can change this. It is far beyond our reach."

"When the people of Paris had enough, they stormed the Bastille and many things changed. This can happen again."

Impressed with his ability to speak so well about the rights and financial obligations of the local farmers, Josephine began to see Paul regularly. Her mother was impressed by his ownership of so much fertile land, but she didn't realize that he was somewhat of a firebrand as well. Such voices of dissent were always risky, but fortunately the Schaeffers were not involved in politics, so Paul's activities were unknown to them when he asked for their daughter's hand in marriage.

Soon after they married, Josephine gave birth to a girl she named Florentine. Paul continued to step up his activities as the movement gained momentum in Alsace. Paul was often away from the farm, which did not help their economic security, but she knew he was working hard for their welfare.

After a long absence, Paul returned to the farm excited about the political movement that he promised would have a beneficial impact on their welfare. "Just think, Josephine—if all our farmers come together to revolt against the seizing of our produce, the police can't arrest us all."

"But they'll arrest you, Paul. You're their leader. I'm not comfortable with that, and our fields are in need of care. There's manure to spread and ground to turn. How can you support the farm when you're always off seeking political support?"

"I have to do this, Josephine. They listen to me. They trust me too. Nobody else can lead them."

"No one else can care for our farm and family either. You'll have to choose soon, I'm afraid. You can't be successful in both endeavors."

"It won't be long now. Change is coming, and it's the farmers that will begin the revolt."

"And the government will put all the leaders in the Bastille, which may include you, Paul. Then what will I do all alone here?"

"I am a nobody. Certainly I am a voice for the farmers but not big enough to concern the police."

"Perhaps you were once a nobody, but now they know you and your followers. I don't see a good end here."

It was 1851 when news reached Obernai.

Two men rode hard from town, their horses spattered with foam when they arrived at the Krach farm. The dogs alerted Paul of their arrival and he came outside to wait for them.

"They protested in the city square; there must have been a hundred men there. Then the soldiers came," one man announced as he directed his mount to the water trough in the yard.

"The soldiers began shooting," the other said. He was a distant cousin of the Krach family who came along to make sure Paul and his family were safe.

Paul sagged against the door frame as he realized the revolt was put down by the government. "How many were lost?"

"We fled the moment they began to fire the rifles. We had to warn you and others. The soldiers will be here in due time, and then who knows what will happen, Paul. They know who you are. They have a list that includes all of us."

"You'd better get ready to go because they'll arrest you or worse," the cousin added, then roughly turned his horse and the two messengers headed out of the yard and on past the Krach farm to bring warnings to other families in the area.

Josephine was standing just inside the door listening to the conversation. They were surely going to arrest him because the government was seeking all those who supported this revolt. Paul had no choice but to leave France immediately or risk arrest and possible execution.

"We'll find a new life in Louisiana," he explained to a tearful Josephine as she quickly packed up his clothing. "I'll go first and find us a place to live, and then I'll send word for you and the children to come and join me. They speak French in New Orleans, and that will help us with a fresh start."

"Do they have farms in that city?"

"I can't say, but many of our countrymen have immigrated there, and there is a whole quarter of the city where the French expatriates are living. Perhaps there will be families from Alsace. It's so hard to go without you, my love, and leave behind our beautiful daughter, but I know you are strong enough to take care of everything. It won't be a long wait. I promise."

They said tearful good-byes on the quay in Marseilles. They clung to each other, fully aware that this might be their last moment together. "I'll find work and rent a house. Come as soon as you can after the baby is born," Paul said.

Paul placed his hand on his wife's swollen belly, kissed her, and then bent down to pick up his toddler daughter. "I want you to take care of your *Maman*, my little Florentine. You must help her every day."

"But you have so little money, Paul. How will we pay for the passage?" his wife asked.

"I'll send it to you once I find employment. I'm young and strong. What I save will be enough for a start," he reassured her.

Paul hugged his wife again, her tears staining his waistcoat. "Dry your tears. Don't let the girl see you weeping. This is a happy occasion. It's the beginning of our new life, and my only regret is that you can't come with me, but this cattle ship is no place for a woman in your condition."

The journey across the Atlantic and into the tempestuous Caribbean

Pauline Schaeffer, youngest daughter of Mama Dejan, spent only a short time in New Orleans and then returned to France to marry Emil Biche. The offspring of this marriage would include Andre Lebert, who began the European section of the Esnard genealogy.

was hazardous in a good year, and by the time they landed at the levee in New Orleans, Paul was visibly thinner. Despite his life as a farmer, he was certain he would never spend another day in the company of livestock. During that time at sea he realized how arduous it would be starting over again so far from home. But, he reminded himself, it was far more preferable than being bled dry by the government or dying by guillotine.

Josephine named the new baby girl Pauline, after her absent father. Pauline was christened in the Dinsheim cathedral with Josephine's parents and cousins in attendance. Afterward they all returned to the Schaeffer home for refreshments.

"It's been months since he left, and there's no word from him," Josephine explained to her mother and aunts while the men were outside drinking wine. "He said he'd write as soon as he arrived, and now it's already a year."

"Perhaps his ship sank, or it's possible he arrived and has not yet settled," her mother said, keeping a pleasant face for her daughter.

"Even if he didn't find work, he could at least send a letter. This is what concerns me most. I dare not use our meager savings to go and find him because there would be nothing left here for the girls."

"Your father feels the same way. He asked me if you might consider a proposal. He and some other family members are hoping to invest what money they have in Louisiana since there is so little return here now. If you must go to find Paul, perhaps you can carry this money with you to invest for us at higher interest or return."

Josephine ruminated on this proposal. "So I will become your agent in Louisiana?"

"That's correct. Many others in our family are unhappy with how things are here, and we don't see much change in the future. We were hoping Paul could help us with such investments, but that is obviously out of the question. Since you need to find Paul, we'll pay for your passage and lodging as our agent. We'll take care of Florentine and Pauline for you until you find Paul or at least obtain a position yourself."

Like many nights before, Josephine couldn't sleep, disaster scenarios whirling in her head. Shipwreck, disease, robbers, and a dozen other unsavory conclusions made it difficult to relax. She struggled with the promising Schaeffer proposition, but she would be forced to be separate from her children, which she resisted with every fiber of her being. But they had to do something. With Paul gone a year, despair dogged her every hour of the day. The farm was going to ruin and she was not able to hire men because she had no income. Perhaps it was time to sell the land, she pondered as her eyelids grew heavy, but she dared not without Paul's blessing.

Josephine contemplated the most difficult decision of her life.

It was bitterly cold in late February. Josephine spent much of her days alone in the damp, dark stateroom with its single tiny porthole. A ticket in steerage gave her little more than a closet for the crossing. As she lay listening to the groaning belly of the ship, dread overwhelmed her. There were too many unknowns, she realized. Despite her rather substantial valise of family money, Josephine worried about this curious new-world city and how she, a single woman, could get along on her own. Inside her heart where the love for her daughters had swelled, there was merely a dark, empty hole. Many times she wondered if she'd made the right decision to leave them behind with the Schaeffers, but when she looked around at her current condition, she couldn't imagine the girls cooped up in such a small, inhospitable space. While darkness shrouded her days, the separation from her babies haunted every sleepless night.

The only bright side of the passage was becoming friends with the captain, who had grown up along the Normandy coast. He recognized her accent with its occasional hints of German dialect and invited her to dine with him one evening.

Josephine wore her only good dress, a dark violet bodice with a narrow skirt, very simple and somber. At the table, she eventually passed the small talk to express her concerns about the best place for woman alone in the foreign city.

"When you arrive, go straight to St. Louis Cathedral," the captain said. "I know the priests there. They are French Jesuits, and they always ask me to bring them wine from home. I have three cases from the Rhineland in my hold right now. You'll know the cathedral; it's the tallest steeple in town and sits on the main square. I have heard they are most helpful to immigrants from their homeland."

"Would they help me find my husband too?"

"I'm sure they would, though there's no way to know if your spouse ever reached the city much less attended Mass there."

"That's the problem; I just don't know. He didn't send a single letter since his departure, which was over a year ago."

The captain's face fell and Josephine prodded him. "Why do you look so sad?"

The captain paused, thinking over what he was about to say.

"My dear, New Orleans is a city of fevers, particularly in the summer. There is always sickness. Some years are worse than others."

"My husband was a very strong man."

"There was an epidemic of yellow fever last year. It was the worst in my memory because the river was very high and there was much flooding. Hundreds, maybe thousands, died. I know this because the city was quarantined so we couldn't drop anchor in New Orleans. Instead we sailed upriver to Baton Rouge."

"So you're saying that Paul may be sick and that's why he didn't write?"

"Who can say? I am just stating the fact that according to your departure date for him, he arrived just before that epidemic. The Ursuline Sisters tended the sick, and the priests at St. Louis came often to their hospital to give the last rites. Some of them became infected and they died too. They won't know if your husband is among the dead, but the priests often help French-speaking immigrants. Go there and you may learn something."

Josephine told herself over and over that Paul could not have died in the epidemic because he was so strong and full of life. She dared not give the epidemic a second thought, for fear the darkness of uncertainty would overtake her nights altogether.

When Josephine's ship tied up at the levee in New Orleans, the strange city was whirling around the celebration of Carnival, held the week before the beginning of Lent. This forty-day period of fast and abstinence began on Ash Wednesday. The day before, known as Fat Tuesday, would end a week-long series of celebrations and parades. As Catholics, the Schaeffers of Alsace had always prepared for the austerity of Lent too, but their modest festivities were nothing like this wild debauchery. The streets were packed with people, many of the women wearing *tignons* of brightly-colored cloth wrapped creatively upon their heads. The vivid fabrics contrasted with so many shades of tea-colored complexions. As an immigrant from cool Northeastern France, Josephine had never seen African people before.

She left her things on the wharf and wove her way through the merrymakers, avoiding the sticky black mud by keeping to the wood sidewalks when she could. Just as the captain had said, the cathedral spire indeed stood well above the rooftops of the French Quarter. By the time she reached the square, her shoes and the hem of her dress were black with mud.

Josephine was ushered into the rectory by an old priest who spoke to her in that familiar German-tinged dialect of her homeland.

"I am Father Bourg, my dear. Please, come inside."

He gave her a comfortable chair in the sitting room and asked the black housekeeper to bring tea. Josephine sat demurely across from the father as he poured from an ornate silver pot, the tea calming her like a gentle hug from her mother.

"This isn't a place for a French woman to be by herself, Madame," he began, his tone disapproving. Josephine could only imagine how he'd react if he learned she'd left her baby daughters behind.

"My husband is lost, and I need to find him quickly," she explained, choking back her tears.

"Do you know how many ships deliver immigrants to this city every day? To find one Frenchman may be quite difficult if he is not listed as a member of our parish. Would you like me to check while you enjoy your tea?"

"Oh, yes, Father. I have nowhere else to go."

"You say he sailed in 1828?"

"Yes. In the early spring."

Just as Josephine finished her second cup of tea Father Bourg returned. She knew by his expression that the search was a failure. Paul was not known at the cathedral.

"*Madame*, don't despair. There's a chance he's known at one of the smaller churches around the edge of the city. Perhaps at Sacred Heart?"

"Thank you, *Père*. But until then I must find inexpensive lodging. My things are sitting on the levee and I have no place to sleep tonight."

Father Bourg merely shook his head. She in turn studied his long gray beard and threadbare cassock. This was not a wealthy priest by any means, she thought. Yet that made him all the more dear to her for he would understand the depths of her plight. Finally his face brightened. "Ah, there may be employment for you, and it would offer lodging and work in a safe place. Come, let us pay a visit to Monsieur Schmidt."

Josephine's heart leapt at the first bit of good news since Paul left home.

"I officiated over the funeral of Monsieur Schmidt's wife, who died in childbirth last month. So very sad it was. Now there are three small children without their mother. The maid is busy enough keeping the household. A wet nurse is caring for the infant. They need a governess to teach the children in French and help them learn their manners and deportment. Can you do that, Madame?"

Agreeing it was a perfect place for at least a temporary stay, Josephine and Father Bourg took a cab from the busy downtown Cathedral to a quiet residential neighborhood farther from the riverfront. They stopped before a three-story brick townhouse with tall windows framed in striking white. Across the street was a large open space shaded by trees, the ground packed hard.

"A park?" Josephine asked, recalling that day when she'd first heard Paul speak in Dinsheim, a manicured park that was not at all similar to this rustic area.

"No, not a park, Madame. That's Congo Square," the priest explained. "Slaves who work in the city go there each Sunday to dance. It is quite a sight and reminds me of my mission days on the West African coast."

The priest helped Josephine step out of the cab onto the banquette in front of the house, then instructed the driver to wait so he could return to the Cathedral. They stepped up to the porch and Father Bourg lifted the knocker on the tall front doors. Soon rapid, echoing footsteps approached within the house upon what sounded like wood floors. A thin, black woman opened the door.

"Father Bourg! What a pleasant surprise," she said, then stepped back for them to enter. "Monsieur Schmidt is at home today. Please come in."

Josephine was amazed at the beautiful interior of the brick home, its high ceilings decorated with plaster filigree illuminated windows so tall light flooded into the sitting room. The maid gestured for them to be seated upon an elegant settee, then she disappeared down the hallway to the kitchen.

Josephine was instantly impressed by the tall man who greeted them as if they were gentry, not a farm wife and an old missioner. Schmidt was middle-aged and well dressed, yet she could see the grief of losing a spouse in his eyes. They would eventually share this same emotional ground of losing a loved one and being forced to go on without the other parent for the children. Mr. Schmidt sat across from them in a velvet-lined easy chair, his slender legs crossed to reveal well-made shoes.

"Now what can I do for you?" he said in the strong articulate voice of a prominent lawyer.

"The young lady, Madame Krach, is in need of lodging and employment. She speaks French and can read and write too. She is hoping to find her husband, who may be in this city or may have never arrived. There are no clues to his disposition."

"Then you don't know if he's alive still?"

"No," Josephine said in her most cultured voice. "He wished to immigrate to New Orleans with all of us, but there were complications."

"Not unusual these days. Things in Europe are unsettled to say the least, but alas, it's always been that way in Alsace. My father was an immigrant too. He came to Louisiana early on during the Revolution, so things were similar for him as for your husband. But my father's family was forced to flee because they were known at court. I was born here in New Orleans after they settled, which made me an American citizen."

Such openness established a common bond between Josephine and her employer, but she never admitted to the priest or Schmidt that she was carrying a vast amount of money.

Once her bags were brought from the levee, Josephine settled in with the Schmidt family and went to work. Despite her new lodging, she remained sad and despondent at her state of affairs. Whenever there was a bit of time to herself, the footman hitched up the buggy and drove her to another Catholic church in the city. The slave waited while she inquired if Paul was among their parishioners. She had no success. Not a single person had ever heard of him.

Josephine learned more about the yellow fever epidemic from Monsieur Schmidt and the colored staff. It had paralyzed New Orleans that summer after Paul had sailed. "It was sad to see so many European immigrants die so soon after arriving here," Schmidt had said in one of their conversations, always in fluent French. "They were ill prepared for the heat, and lodgings were few. Many simply expired on the banquette, and left until the slaves were sent to gather them."

So many died that year that the graveyards were overflowing with bodies. The stench was unremitting. Schmidt explained to Josephine that "Here in New Orleans, groundwater lies so close to the surface of the ground, we can't bury our dead in the earth. In years of flood, coffins buried underground literally float to the surface. It is a most gruesome situation."

"So what did they do with the dead?"

"In the end they had to burn the bodies, with most of them so distorted that identification was impossible. Mass graves were out of the question because even a shallow hole would fill with water moments after it was dug. But the larger problem here was fear of contamination. The slaves were so afraid of touching the dead that only the lash would drive them collect and burn these remains. Few people left their houses for weeks on end. They kept the windows shut against the miasma from the bayou that carries disease. Every night they burned tar on the street corners to kill disease and drive out mosquitoes, which were particularly ferocious due to so much high water. I took no risks with my family. We fled to Charleston because the smell of burning tar on the street corners was overwhelming."

After learning that awful truth, Josephine maintained her dignity in public but cried secretly in the darkness for the bright young man she'd loved—and likely lost. She was now alone. She would have to find a great deal of strength within herself to go on because returning to France was out of the question. Not only did she lack the funds for another passage, but letters from her family said there had been soldiers at the house looking for both her and Paul, just as the cousin had warned. If she did go home she would surely be arrested for treason.

In that first year in New Orleans, Josephine Schaeffer Krach would thank God for the Schmidt children who kept her mind off her plight. She was alone in a strange and deadly city with no means of supporting herself. She wrote short concise letters to her family in Dinsheim, and with every word the hole in her heart only grew larger. The search for Paul bore no fruit. Josephine had but one conclusion: she was now a widow.

PART III

THE ESNARDS

ETIENNE ENARD

New Orleans, 1800

E TIENNE HAD LEARNED HIS TRADE IN FRANCE, APPRENticed since boyhood to his father, Pierre, in the family business. Pierre was a master craftsman well known in Nance for fine furniture that would often find its way to the drawing rooms of Paris. Before Etienne reached full journeyman status, the Revolution had destroyed the demand for quality work as the nobility either left France or were executed. Both Etienne and his brother, Pierre Charles, saw no future in their hometown. With so many of their former customers fleeing to America and the Caribbean, the young men were encouraged to follow. Demand for stylish continental furniture would continue in the New World as more French left the upheaval of Napoleon's Empire.

The young carpenter watched surveyors divide the plantation lands of Philippe de Marigny de Mandeville into a new subdivision in 1805. It would become a *faubourg*, or suburb, on the east side of the old French Quarter, offering new homes for the city's rapidly growing population of immigrants. Unlike the old city where Etienne lived at the time, these new blocks were composed of much larger, deeper lots with alleys behind that would be far more conducive to the kind of business he had in mind. He kept a sharp eye out for a building with a sizeable storefront, and behind that a very large workshop and loading dock at the rear on the alley.

Many fellow craftsmen in New Orleans were old merchants and Creoles who had provided their services to the city for generations. They all hoped Marigny would result in a community free of the spatial and social constraints of an old city. Here Etienne could work close to those who supplied his raw materials such as lumber, hardware, upholstery, and delivery services.

30

The rift between the brothers began the moment they arrived in New Orleans. Etienne enjoyed the journey with Pierre Charles, and they talked often about their plans for a workshop and business in their new home free of their father's critical eye. Though Etienne had trained Pierre Charles to help him with the work, he never felt the same love of wood as Etienne did. This offered the perfect partnership: one brother focused on making money and the other in charge of creating quality products.

From that first day, Pierre Charles had become enchanted with the women of New Orleans. Those mixed-race beauties called "high yellow" with their *café au lait* skin tones and almond-shaped eyes captivated him. Etienne soon realized that his brother had lost his focus. Business was secondary to him now, and Pierre Charles made no effort to locate suitable lodgings or a workshop. Instead he was drawn to the bars and cafes where the beautiful mulatto women were eager to pass the time with a handsome young Frenchman.

With his partner compelled to go elsewhere, Etienne's dreams faded. To get by, Etienne took jobs in local carpentry shops to learn more about the trade in their new land. Though they still shared a room, Pierre Charles had taken up the absinthe habit and had begun smoking strong American cigars. Finally abandoning all self-control, Pierre finally left to take up residence in a seedy part of town with a colored woman and her mother. The girl gave birth to a son just a few months later and died soon afterward.

Pierre had no interest in the child. Just after the poor woman expired, he was out in the taverns seeking new companionship because the girl's mother immediately sent him packing. Days later, he showed up at Etienne's workplace to announce that the infant had been delivered to the Ursuline Convent Orphanage.

"Can't that girl's mother continue to care for the child?" Etienne asked, exasperated at his brother's lack of feeling for his own son.

"She is old and they say she has a cancer."

"Then find work and hire a nurse, Pierre. It is your child, your only child."

"You haven't seen him, Etienne. The boy is even darker than his mother. If I claim him, no white woman would ever marry me—should I find one with enough dowry to make it worthwhile."

"It is a mortal sin to abandon your baby. You'd better go to confession."

"It is also a mortal sin to have a child out of wedlock, little brother. So which is the greater sin? To create the child or to give him up to good sisters who will raise him properly? I have done the right thing, to be sure."

Etienne felt different about the boy who was an Enard by birth. His parents in Nance would have been heartbroken to know their grandchild was literally given away. Certainly there was a stigma around having a colored son, but it was nothing compared to the lifelong guilt of failing to protect an innocent.

The sisters wore long white habits that seemed to Etienne the most unsuitable clothing one could possibly find for their tropical climate. How they kept the linen stiff and starched in high humidity remained a mystery. A young sister brought the baby out wrapped in swaddling clothes, the nun's cheeks flushed with the afternoon's heat. She smiled, her face melting into one nearly as innocent as the baby she held, and she whispered, "Thank you, Monsieur," as she handed him over. "The Lord will reward you for this."

Etienne took the child back to the new building he had leased on Marigny Street, where small living quarters were integrated into its rooms. He hired a nurse to care for the boy and cook for him as he set about the great task of setting up his workshop. Though Etienne had not planned to take on such a great responsibility, something in his heart grew large as he watched the boy sleep in a makeshift cradle, a deep bottom drawer freshly made for a highboy he was working on.

Gabrielle Simeon Enard was six years old in 1810 when Etienne's business grew into one of the better establishments in Marigny. Pierre Charles still lived in a rooming house in the heart of the Quarter and only came to see them when he was on the verge of eviction. The shop became Simeon's schoolroom, where he learned from an early age the secrets of French carpentry and proved equally as good with his small hands as his grandfather Pierre back home in Nance. But Simeon preferred playing in the alley with the other children of the neighborhood, most of them swarthy as he was, many considerably darker, but few bore the same coarse black hair that had marked the Esnards of Nance.

Etienne built an excellent clientele that trusted his recommendations on stylish fabrics and trim to create perfectly matched settees and footed chairs for their parlors. The wives often came just to marvel over the latest imported upholstery fabrics and to browse Etienne's furniture design books shipped directly from Paris. Etienne's early years watching his father work with the French nobility gave him a special ability to appeal to those wealthy land owners who had fled the Revolution. Word had spread to planters upriver of his shop and his beautiful work.

Etienne needed more assistance in the showroom so he could devote himself exclusively to his craft. He felt a woman's touch would appeal to his growing clientele of wealthy, free colored merchants and immigrants. The wives sought to achieve the same stylish households as their equals in white society, and a female salesperson would be the best way to serve them.

Late one afternoon after work had ceased earlier than normal, Etienne's friends and associates drifted into the shop with cheese, bread, and choice bottles of French wine. It had become their custom to gather at week's end to relax and share the news.

"I have made a decision," Etienne announced after he poured drinks for all his friends. "I must find a beautiful woman to work for me."

"The red-light district isn't far," one portly ironworker chided. The men roared with laughter.

"No, I honestly need someone who can take care of my female customers. They need a woman's sensibility when they come here. I've seen how well this can work when others have done the same. But this woman, she must be fluent in both English and French."

"Oh, now he wants an *educated* woman from the red-light district!" Again the men roared and wine flowed.

Frustrated, Etienne threw up his hands and moved on to other subjects. But later, after the men drifted home in the dark, his tailor, a small thin man, remained behind, finishing off the last of the burgundy.

"I know who might help you, and you know her too," he said. "Madame Felix is a fine seamstress, and her daughters are already trained to work with the American women and *gens de couleur* equally well. Perhaps one of them would suit you?"

Etienne recalled the woman he'd hired to do his mending; she returned each piece of clothing repaired, washed, and pressed to perfection. Her young daughters helped with the work and made simple repairs, sewed buttons, made deliveries, and purchased supplies. They had to deal with the difficult white female customers who purchased their elaborate gowns in fine silk and lace with brocades and embroideries.

One Sunday after Mass, Etienne walked over to Madame Felix's house, which doubled as her place of business. It was a squat Creole cottage that was far older than it looked. Madame Felix answered the door, her hair tied up in a tignon the color of a fresh peach, which brought out the richness of her skin tone.

"Why, Monsieur Enard, I don't have anything for you today, or have you forgotten?" she said.

"No, this isn't about laundry. I have a proposal for you. May I come inside?"

"Of course, Monsieur, but you'll have to find a chair. We're preparing dresses for a wedding and there's lace everywhere!"

Etienne stepped cautiously to a Windsor chair next to the empty fireplace.

"So what can I do for you, Monsieur Enard?"

"I'm in need of a beautiful woman," he blurted, then, realizing how that sounded, he stopped and rephrased. "With the Americans, their wives and mothers decide what they put in their homes. I believe I could sell a great deal more if there was a woman in my shop who appealed to their way of thinking. Call it a female touch."

"You are a smart man, Etienne. This is how I train my daughters because the city is growing and they are talking about subdividing the Tremé Plantation and that means more homes with more women who need dresses and furniture."

"Perhaps one of your daughters would be suitable, provided she speaks English well enough."

"Ah, that's easy. Marie, my oldest, could be suitable because she speaks French, and her English is improving every day. That girl won't remain here much longer because she's not a seamstress and refuses to do laundry. She'll have to find another endeavor to support herself."

"I met Marie before when she delivered the laundry last year."

"Ah yes, deliveries. She'd drop them off, sneak away with her book, then return too late in the day for another delivery. I warn you, that girl has a head on her shoulders, but that's not what I need. Here, nimble fingers and a quiet mind—that is most valuable for dressmakers."

"May I speak with her?"

Madame Felix rang a small bell that hung on a cord around her neck. Immediately three faces peeked through the curtain behind her, proving they'd been listening all along. Then one stepped forward, the other two vanishing again. Marie nimbly stepped through the crowded room so her skirt would not disturb any of the lace pieces or thin paper patterns. Her tall stature and thin frame lent a certain grace that immediately appealed to Etienne.

"*Bonjour*, Monsieur Enard. So you are seeking an assistant?"

It was a simple thing for Marie Felix to move into Etienne's apartments at the shop. Marie was well trained and soon proved her worth by encouraging Etienne's style-conscious customers to invest in higher-quality imported fabrics and the latest Empire designs from the continent. She arrived at work each day in clothing created by her mother's nimble fingers, and every sale earned her a generous commission that paid for the fabrics.

It was close to Christmas when Pierre Charles unexpectedly appeared outside the shop one day. His clothing was disheveled and it was obvious he hadn't shaved or cut his hair in months. Pierre stood out on the banquette there for a long time, spitting tobacco between swallows from his tin hip flask. Etienne was out running errands.

Marie frowned as she peeked through a shuttered window at the man defiling their stoop with tobacco. Irritated, she opened the door and stood blocking the opening. "Monsieur, please move along. I don't want to clean this sidewalk again today."

Pierre Charles glared at the beautiful woman occupying his brother's shop. "Where is Etienne?"

"Monsieur Enard is down on Canal at the moment, but he will be back in an hour or so. Who can I say called on him?"

"Who do you think I am?"

"From what I can see from your manners, you aren't from this neighborhood."

Just then Marie felt the touch of Simeon hiding behind her broad skirts, his little body shaking curiously. Concerned she turned and said, "Simeon, please come out from behind me and greet this man politely."

The school-age boy refused, then retreated into the dark shop. Simeon was always eager to meet visitors and rarely afraid of anything except perhaps the planters who came to town to visit their colored families. Simeon had heard rumors they killed people of color without a second thought and were never prosecuted for it.

"I'm sorry, sir," Marie explained. "The boy has better manners than that."

"Forget the boy. I would like to take you down to Bourbon Street right now and buy you a pretty bobble to hang on that slender neck of yours."

Marie didn't reveal her anger at such a bold suggestion. "Monsieur Enard prefers I remain here until he returns," she said in a clipped voice.

"Who are you to say no to me?" he said in a deep voice as he reached for the buttons on the front of her dress, but Marie drew back violently, knowing exactly what was on his mind. Pierre lunged again, trying to get through the doorway, but already Marie was closing it upon the worn toe of his battered boot. Pierre fought her, but the girl was strong from so many years at the washboard.

Finally Marie was able to slam the door shut and lock it securely. She turned to find Simeon crouched behind a china cabinet, his eyes wide with tears. "Oh, *mon petit chéri*," she said, gathering the boy into her arms. "Why are you so afraid of that man? He's nobody to us."

"That is Uncle Pierre. He always asks Papa for money. Last time he wanted enough to buy a slave woman off the block. I am glad you wouldn't let him in."

Just then, Etienne walked in the back door from the alley. He immediately noticed that both his boy and Marie were frightened.

"Papa," Simeon cried, running to his father and hugging him tightly. "Pierre has come back again, but Marie wouldn't let him in. She pushed him out!"

"Good for her. Marie, keep yourself far away from him. Though he's my brother, the man is not sane and very dangerous."

From that day forward, Marie strived to help Simeon come to terms with his biological father, Pierre Charles. For Marie, this was not difficult because her own father was a white planter from the delta country. He had freed all of the women of his illegitimate colored family before he died many years before. The planter never married Madame Felix, but such unions were commonplace.

In time Marie would become more than an employee. She came to love Simeon dearly and lavished her attention on the boy. Etienne found her ways deeply comforting because his boy finally had a mother-like figure. But it was her beauty and intelligence that soon captured Etienne's heart too. Though they could never marry, Marie moved her things to Etienne's apartments, and they would live like every other white man with a colored wife in the city.

In time Etienne Enard's furniture, upholstery, and fabric shop became a place where many trades met: the lumber brokers, millwrights, hardware dealers, and upholsterers. Soon they organized into an unofficial guild that furnished the houses of the city and rural plantations along the Great River Road. The lavish profits of these enormous cotton and sugarcane farms, tended by an army of black slave labor, fed the planter's families, and these poured cash into New Orleans for the goods and services they desired.

By age twenty-six, Simeon had mastered the work and became a full-fledged cabinetmaker. This was the year Etienne began to complain of pain in his abdomen. The old man was almost sixty and his work slowed, though he was obsessed with designing new pieces for his wealthiest and most influential clients. Even with a limited workload, the occasional grippe had grown more frequent, becoming particularly acute whenever Etienne drank wine. Good European burgundy was his greatest enjoyment, and he would not give it up, imbibing until the fire in his belly was too great to endure.

Finally the doctor was called. After a thorough examination, he concluded that Etienne's liver was failing, probably due to a waterborne parasite, which was not uncommon due to contamination from flooding. Soon the old man's eyes showed yellow jaundice, and then it spread to his fingernails.

Ever the opportunist, the moment Pierre Charles heard about his brother's illness, he returned to the store. This time he was even more unkempt, his clothing filthy and reeking of alcohol. He pounded on the door, demanding Marie let him in to see his brother. Reluctantly she opened the door, then, without saying a word, she gestured for him to enter and pointed to a chair. Then she disappeared through the showroom and workshop to the living quarters behind. Not wanting Pierre to see how weak he was, Marie helped Etienne sit up, combed his hair, and put his shoes beside the edge of the bed. By the time Pierre was summoned, Etienne appeared to be in far better health.

"Have you written a will, Etienne?" Pierre asked immediately after pleasantries were exchanged.

"I hear you've become somewhat of an expert at probate," Etienne said, his voice dripping with sarcasm.

Pierre smiled, revealing his yellow, cracked teeth. "I was merely a facilitator helping my customers get money quickly."

"Are you here to facilitate my estate too?"

"Perhaps I can help you file the papers. After all, you can't leave it to Marie because she's colored, and Simeon isn't your natural son. The way I see it, you have no heirs."

"So why not wait for probate to take its course after I'm gone?"

"The lawyers say I must prove our affiliation and that of our brothers and sisters in France. It could take a year or more to obtain the affidavits from home."

"Then let it be so."

Pierre Charles's hair was now gray, the edges of his beard were brown from nicotine, and his fingernails were too long. He slowly moved about the room, studying Etienne's private belongings as though he was taking an inventory himself. "But if I was curator, if you designated me as such, it would be much simpler."

"For whom, Pierre? Me or you?"

Frustrated, Pierre Charles didn't reply but simply snapped his walking stick under his arm and left in a huff. He would go home to his desk and begin writing letters to speed the process of determining the heirs to his brother's estate. Pierre had debts, and those who demanded payment were not banks or landlords but a group of men who bought light-skinned pubescent girls from the plantations and put them on their backs in the cribs of the city. They were not the merciful type, and Pierre had run up a good deal of credit in their bawdy houses and gambling parlors.

According to Napoleonic laws of that day, Etienne's estate would be

This 1822 probate record includes succession of Etienne Enard to his brother Pierre Charles Enard and affidavits sent from France establishing all their siblings and parents living at the time.

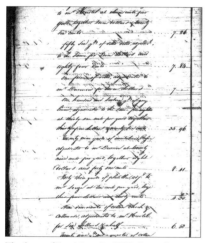

The laws of Louisiana in 1822 deemed anyone who dies intestate must have the estate inventoried for dissolution before distribution to siblings and children if they exist. This inventory was so detailed that it became quite clear what Etienne carried in his store and the kind of work done there.

spread evenly among his brothers and sisters. Pierre knew that would require selling the shop and its contents. But what concerned him most of all was that every day that passed, Marie could be quietly selling their merchandise and personal property item by item until hardly anything was left for probate. That meant little reward for him in the end.

Etienne Enard died of liver failure in 1822 with Marie and Simeon at his side. Marie was so distraught that there was no comfort for her agony at losing her lover. She knew also that she was on her own now, and though she had never enjoyed the protection of marriage, the white man who loved and cared for her was gone. Now she was among the many older colored women who had lost their mates without the benefit of marriage. They were destined to get by on what they could earn in menial jobs. Fortunately Etienne had directed Marie and Simeon to remove what there was of value from the store so it would never go to Pierre Charles.

In those weeks after Etienne's death, new streaks of gray glittered in Marie's raven hair. She knew Pierre Charles would fight her for everything he could. If the past was any indication of the future, what money Pierre did inherit from the eventual sale of his brother's store was likely to be spent on drink and women.

SIMEON ENARD

New Orleans, 1822

IMEON MISSED HIS FATHER DEEPLY. IT PAINED HIM TO
see Etienne's shop inventoried and sold for pennies on the dollar. Pierre
Charles, thin and wild-eyed, stood around like a vulture watching every
move, his attitude betraying no sadness at the loss of his brother. He had
finally been made curator of the estate, which thrilled him to no end. Already
he was accumulating new debts in anticipation of his share of the proceeds.
Because Simeon was illegitimate and Marie was colored, there was no indication any of it would go to them under Pierre's prevue.

Marie lived with Simeon after Etienne's funeral. Her efforts to find work
were not successful, and with each disap-
pointment she fell deeper into depression
and grief. Some days she failed to leave
her bed at all. What money she had was
rapidly disappearing, and soon she'd be
broke.

On his way to work, Simeon trudged
down an alley behind Esplanade on the
way to a favorite baker in Tremé for the
day's bread. He passed an old black man
working inside a dusty barn, the double
doors wide open to catch the breeze. The
man was pushing a wood plane over flat
boards of freshly milled bald cypress as
smoothly as a bow flies over violin strings.

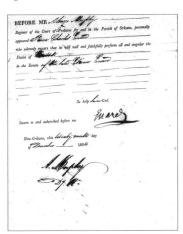

This 1830 signature page drawn up by
Alonzo Morphy, probate court registrar,
designates Pierre Charles as the executor of Etienne Enard's estate and includes
Pierre's actual signature. This would be
the earliest link between the Esnard and
Morphy family.

39

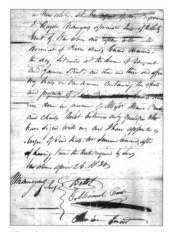

This document drawn up upon the death of Pierre Charles Enard details his final possessions within a single armoire and no other personal property. It's signed at the bottom by Simeon Enard himself, the only living kin and beneficiary.

Simeon paused to admire the beautiful grain of that wood, derived from ancient-growth trees that filled the bayous around New Orleans. Those oddly humanlike knees that rose above the waterline around the great trunks gave them an eerie presence in the dark water. Simeon realized at that moment that he really didn't want to work in the French style of his father. The gilt hardware and exotic woods were simply no match for the sight and aroma of this bayou tree that was famously resistant to termites and rot.

The old man paused the plane, then squatted down to eyeball the level surface. He took an ash brush and swept the dust off the surface and eyeballed it again. Then he brushed it one more time before turning slowly toward Simeon, still standing outside.

"I'm sorry about your *père*," the old man said. "He was a good man."

"You knew my father?"

"For a long time, *c'est si bon*. I know you from the guild meetings. I am Batiste."

Simeon stepped into the shaded workroom to shake Batiste's rock-hard, calloused hand.

"Where will you work now that they've closed the shop?"

"I don't know. I would like to open my own workshop, but I have no money. My uncle didn't give us anything, not a single *sou*."

"*Mon Dieu*," Batiste whispered. "Pierre was downtown spending like a drunken sailor last week. The man has no morals. Me, I started up from nothin' and will take even less with me when I die. My old massa taught me how to work wood. He was a good man and bought my freedom. Long gone now. Jus' me alone. Have you any tools?"

"My daddy took them out of the shop before he died so I am ready to work. I could go to one of the fine shops, but my eye likes that table there, and that's all I want to do—cypress work. It's a part of this place. Maybe a part of me too."

"Come on in here then and feel this one," Batiste said, stepping back from his work.

Simeon let his fingers lightly slide across the rock-hard cypress.

"That wood will never go away," Batiste added. "That tree's as old as God and it'll last forever. What I make, boy, live long after I'm gone. It still be here for yo' children and yo' children's children."

Simeon walked outside with Batiste, who cradled his right arm. "Damned thing hurts me night and day." Then he sat in the shade upon a round of wood where the breeze floated through the alley. "If you're willin' to work, I can use you. Go home and get your tools. I'll give you half of every dollar we make. Me, I'm growing very old. The pain in my arm keeps me awake at night. I need someone young and strong to help."

Soon everyone knew that Simeon had become Batiste's partner and was on the way to becoming a master cypress carver. It wasn't long until there was a waiting list for Batiste's work, and they waited for Simeon's too when the time was right.

Marie Felix died less than a year after Etienne passed away. She had grown thin and pale, so weakened that she became feverish at the very start of the hottest summer they could remember. It was certain that cholera would visit the city because water in the shallower wells had declined to just a thin, muddy layer at the bottom. Such conditions were always the harbinger of epidemic.

As the Americans celebrated their independence in the streets of the Quarter with gunfire and rockets, Simeon held his mother as she struggled to drink the water he offered, only to vomit it immediately afterward. Her skin was loose and wrinkled from extreme dehydration, signaling the end was near. The suffering and pain in the gut was unimaginable, and all he could do was pour laudanum down her throat in hopes she would keep it down long enough to sleep.

It was in one of those deep coma-like dream states that Marie Felix slipped away to join Etienne in a heaven where all cloth was silk and the brocades impossibly complex. Simeon cried over his loss, for now he was truly alone. His only remaining parent, Pierre Charles, was sitting in the city jail, charged with threatening to shoot a faro dealer for cheating.

Simeon sat in the stifling room for a whole day and night, coming to terms with his mother's lifeless body. Finally he covered her with an intricate Spanish lace shawl, the one she wore to Mass on holy days.

Devastated, he left her to walk through the revelry to the undertaker's home, and there he notified the mulatto slave that she was ready to be placed in the tomb next to Etienne in St. Louis #6. It was raining when he stepped outside again, and he found himself inextricably drawn to Batiste's shop where the old man was resting, his arm now laced into a thick leather cuff. A bottle of red wine sat on the workbench.

"She gone now?"

Simeon nodded, tears gathering at the corners of his eyes. He wiped them away with his sleeve.

"C'mon ovah here and sit down with me and have a little of this. It'll make you feel betta."

Batiste uncorked the wine and poured it into their two cups that usually held thick French coffee while they worked. He handed one to Simeon then stood. "May her soul fly swiftly to heaven." The two men held their cups high, then drained them.

Then Batiste toasted yet again, saying, "Let us pray to the good Lord this cholera doesn't grow worse. It is a bad year, *mon chérie*, and only God knows who is next."

MARIE LOUISE SMITH-ENARD

WIFE OF SIMEON ENARD, MOTHER OF JEAN BENJAMIN ESNARD

New Orleans, before 1850

ARIE LOUISE WAS BORN IN 1812 JUST AS ANDREW JACKson met the British at the Battle of New Orleans. She was the child of a black woman and a roving American soldier stationed around Algiers, who had come into the city to enjoy its bounty. Marie's mother was unknown, as was the case with many free black women born from slavery. Marie Louise grew up speaking French and was at home in the Marigny within the close-knit community of tradesmen and merchants who were mostly European immigrants and their colored descendants.

Marie Louise passed Etienne Esnard's shop daily on her way to the marketplace. She lived nearby and found the beauty of that window, and those of the dressmakers and jewelers, irresistible. So when Etienne's shop closed, she was truly disappointed because she'd just become aware of a handsome young man working inside. His hair was black and straight and his eyes were such a deep dark brown under heavy brows that they drew her to them. She spent many a night creating fantasies of how she might meet him and what she would say. Marie Louise did not want to seem too forward,

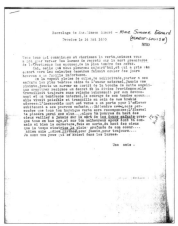

This typewritten copy of the 1850 death of Marie Louise Smith is in French, obtained by Christine Esnard from the papers of her father, Adrien Esnard, DDS. The translation by Andre Lebert indicates she had eleven children. Extrapolating her death and the birth of her last two children, twin boys, shows she passed away soon after their birth.

43

so she took walks through the neighborhood more often than she needed to, hoping to catch a glimpse of him. Should she accidently run into him there or in church, she might be able to coquettishly start up a conversation, and perhaps find out if he had married or not.

Simeon was drenched with sweat after he and Batiste loaded up a large cypress dining table into their wagon just outside the shop. Simeon was shirtless, his golden skin damp with sweat rippling in the sunlight. Marie Louise, wearing long skirts and a bonnet, was on her way to Mass, purposefully passing through the alley where the shop was located, for it was Ascension Thursday, a holy day of obligation. She passed the two men without turning her head, but Simeon stepped out to stop her and tipped his hat, saying simply, "Madame."

When he removed the hat, a lock of thick black hair tumbled down over one of those dark eyes, and Marie Louise's heart skipped a beat. She glanced at him, then quickly looked away before he could see her blush. She continued on without saying a word.

It was midmorning the next time she passed the shop, and Simeon stepped out of the dark barn directly into her path. Simeon fell in love the moment he heard her soft words and her happy smile, which turned his serious countenance into bright childlike joy. Soon afterward they began to spend time together, and Simeon eventually asked for her hand in marriage.

When the pain in his arm became overwhelming, Batiste finally retired and Simeon moved into 14 Craps Street. There he opened his own store to house Marie Louise and their growing brood in the apartments of the same building. It seemed that almost every year Louise would deliver a new child. She was a fine mother and cared for her children with such joy. Many called her *Myrthee*, a French nickname for one who is always happy.

Marie Louise informed Simeon that she was pregnant for the tenth time in the fall of 1849. Though they were both happy, they were concerned that the family had grown too large, but Louise and Simeon could not stop loving each other. Both found foregoing their nightly lovemaking impossible to bear.

This time Marie Louise said the pregnancy was different. After listening to her growing belly, the doctor pronounced that she was to bear twins. In those days twins were always ominous news. Complications of childbirth were the most common cause of death to women, so the couple waited with fear in their hearts that all would go well.

When the time grew near, Marie Louise was so large she couldn't leave her bed, and the needs of her children demanded much of Simeon's time.

Marie Louise grew pale and weak, something she had never known with the earlier pregnancies. They consulted a midwife. The news wasn't good. The woman gave her some herbs.

Her labor began on April 14 and extended through the day, night, and into the following day. The doctor knew the delivery might be breach, and he tried over and over to turn the babies into position. Marie's screams could be heard next door and down the block. Everyone held their breath waiting for the cry of a child to signal it was over. Simeon fretted and the children were strangely quiet. Eventually Marie Louise's cries dwindled, but still the babies did not appear.

When the two tiny boys finally emerged, they were pale and bluish around the lips. Delivery was followed by a gush of blood that the doctor struggled to control. Marie had barely enough strength to turn her head to see the infants pinking up quickly in the hands of a nurse. A group of neighborhood women could be heard praying the rosary in the parlor with the children. A wet nurse was summoned.

Marie Louise survived the delivery but never recovered. She bled slowly for weeks, growing paler by the day until finally she expired amid the flowers of May 1850. Marie Louise Smith-Esnard was just thirty-seven years old.

The whole community was aghast at the loss, not only of such a happy woman, but because Simeon would now be forced to raise nine children and two infants by himself on a carpenter's pay. Neither he nor Marie Louise had any relatives in the city, making his situation particularly grave. He would not consider giving any to the Ursuline Orphanage because Marie Felix had told him the story of his own rescue from the sisters' care. The twin boys, Dominique and Laurent, would go with the wet nurse to her home, where she would be there for them around the clock.

Simeon had no choice but to hire a woman to run the household, one older and strong enough to keep up with the work and the future demands of twin infants. Women from the church came often to deliver food, particularly during holidays. He spent much of his time working as late as lamplight allowed, rising early to begin again the next morning. The only way Simeon could make the pain of Marie Louise's passing fade the slightest bit was to saw bald cypress planks until he was covered in sweat. So often during those days he'd recall old Batiste's words. "This will be a bad year, *mon chérie,* and only God knows what is next."

PART IV

CIVIL WAR

✣

PIERRE DEJAN

1835

T HEY BAPTIZED HIM CLAUDE PIERRE AFTER HIS BIRTH IN December 1835. He was the fourth son of a successful white banker of French ancestry, Jules Dejan. However, Claude Pierre would not be born in his father's fine home in the Quarter. His birth was in a small cottage in Marigny, where his colored mother, Marguerite Doubere, lived. Like so many in the city, his parents never married. Like his brothers, Jules Jr., Victor, and Antoine, Pierre was born illegitimate.

Jules loved Marguerite and had no other woman. He lived at 116 Saint Anne Street, close to the Dueling Oaks and the Alard Plantation, where the lots were large and the neighborhoods were decidedly white. He was comptroller of the Citizens Bank of Louisiana, one of the primary banks that did business with the many cotton and sugarcane planters. They were known to take slaves as collateral on loans, and occasionally they were forced to liquidate these holdings at slave auctions.

The Citizens Bank of Louisiana would carry accounts for free colored depositors. Among them were many with substantial cash and assets in antebellum times. Many were colored merchants of Marigny, where Dejan's four colored sons grew up and remained into adulthood.

Since he was a small boy, Pierre was drawn to beautiful things and proved quite adept at working with his hands. His keen eye was also able to find diamonds in the rough, and that is what drove him to admire the work of Etienne Enard, Batiste, and other craftsmen of the area. Naturally he would come to know Simeon as well.

Pierre was quite unlike his oldest brother, Jules Jr., who was a fine accountant like his father. The problem for Jules was that everyone knew

Marguerite's background because Jules Sr. never married a white woman until long after her death. Jules Jr. was colored and could therefore never work at the bank with his father. Instead he became a successful accountant and bookkeeper in Marigny for many colored merchants. This allowed him to encourage his customers to bank at Citizens, which pleased his father to no end. The family relationship gave colored merchants a sense of security despite Jules Sr. being white, for he was sympathetic and well known in their community. The Dejan brothers convinced many that under their father's watchful eye, their money would be safe.

Unlike Jules, Pierre did not fit well into the business world. His mother understood that and encouraged his artistic endeavors. He proved to have an uncanny ability to buy low at the auction and sell the same piece at considerable profit. With her help, he was able to buy a tiny cottage at 318 Dauphine among a group of tiny lots at the corner of Barracks Street. One block away, Jules Jr. purchased a similar dwelling at 218 Dauphine. Both men plied their modest trades to the colored community. Both places were conveniently close to Marguerite's home.

Soon the newspapers grew busy publishing stories about the uneasy politics between the North and slave-owning states of the South. Abolitionists had grown bolder, and many societies in the large cities such as Boston and New York were growing militant. While the slave trade had been outlawed, the South maintained its slave-supported agricultural system and they weren't willing to give it up.

Gradually, white men in positions of authority and their colored families became more at risk of scrutiny. With war on the horizon, Jules knew that his sons were in jeopardy and tried to help them as best he could without increasing their visibility. In the past, such relationships were not socially acceptable, but not condemned either. As flames of racism were fanned by the national news, criticism of whites fraternizing with people of color became more common.

To protect his sons who could not legally inherit his wealth, Jules Sr. carefully composed his will. He left half of his estate to his brother Octave Dejan. This money would be for Octave to distribute to Jules's illegitimate sons who had no legal claim on their father's estate. This was likely a common practice at the time when a white parent wished to support undocumented, colored heirs. It left no paper trail that could prove Jules had a colored mistress or offspring from her. There would be no cloud cast upon the social status of Jules's friends and relatives. Octave would dole out the money to each heir as needed for school, for a house, or to make investments.

Pierre, the artistic son, did not warrant much of the money, but Octave did help him buy a house and make purchases at the auction. The young man's keen eye knew a good piece of furniture when he saw it, and if the bid was low enough, he made the purchase. Pierre took it home to his little house to repair or refinish that piece to sell to an individual or local store at considerable profit. Like Simeon, Pierre never tired of making wood look beautiful, and he became a well-known figure at the auction house.

Pierre's Dauphine Street cottage was not far from the home of J. B. Schmidt, a prosperous lawyer who had lost his young wife to childbirth. He had hired the widow Josephine Schaeffer-Krach as governess for his children. Josephine and Pierre often crossed paths on the street, but they rarely said a word. After all, she was white and he was clearly a mulatto. But when they finally did stop to comment on the weather or local news, he was pleased that she had no issue with skin color. They found each other's company a great comfort. Josephine often expressed her dissatisfaction with the limited life of a domestic, and Pierre shared his dreams of creating an empire of furniture.

Though they connected on many levels, Josephine and Pierre were different. She was white and had no ambition but to bring her daughters from France. Pierre was raised with more affluence in a far worldlier home. He did own real estate and had money coming from his father's estate. Only the color barrier divided them, but both realized that if they were to join forces, both their problems could be solved.

Pierre was no stranger to his mother Marguerite's plight, but he knew it was another matter altogether for a colored man to marry a white woman. It was against the law. No justice of the peace would ever consider the ceremony no matter how sympathetic to the colored cause he might be.

They took the only course open to them, to seek *un mariage de conscience.* This was a traditional religious sacramental marriage in the Catholic Church that would free them of the sin of adultery if they were to live together as a couple. Such cohabitation without church sanction would constitute a mortal sin and was considered grounds for excommunication, which would bar them both from the communion rail.

Pierre and Josephine consulted Reverend M. Schifferer, the curate of the Holy Trinity Church. He had never performed a marriage of conscience for a white woman, for it was always to benefit a white man and his mulatto mistress or a colored couple. Schifferer finally chose to defy social standards and free the couple's union of sin. On September 11, 1858, Pierre Dejan and Josephine Schaeffer-Krach were married in a quiet ceremony at Holy

Trinity. The Dejans were legitimate in the eyes of the church, the only institution that mattered to these devout Catholics.

They did not celebrate this marriage, for it was best to keep things quiet. Pierre's father would have been no doubt pleased at his son's choice of a white woman, and Octave gave them a sum of money as a wedding present. But Octave warned his nephew it would be seen as a sham, a parody of marriage, and the less visible the couple were, the better. Politics had grown contemptuous, and the white citizens were threatening to secede from the United States altogether. Should that happen, war was sure to follow. He emphasized the fact that the racial issues had grown so acute that the slave-owning white population was willing to send their fathers, sons, and brothers into battle to preserve the status quo.

After they married, Josephine retained her job at the Schmidt house but now went home to Pierre each evening rather than staying with the lawyer's children. Pierre's little house was small, cramped, and smelled of varnish. Wood dust covered every surface, and Josephine took her time rearranging the interior into a better workspace. They also used an alcove in back by the alley to work outdoors when the weather was good. Pierre continued to attend the auction, and Josephine returned home each night only to work late with her husband stripping and varnishing every new piece he brought home.

With no warehouse to store anything, they were forced to sell what they could before moving on to a new piece of furniture. It was not long before their work sped up and their reputation grew for selling quality furnishings at fair prices to well-to-do households. Pierre and Josephine had begun to make substantial profits, which they salted away for her daughters' eventual arrival and the purchase of a storefront.

After they had saved a good deal of money, Pierre and Josephine asked Uncle Octave for more to help them buy another small house on the corner of Barracks and Dauphine Streets. It was one tiny building in a milieu of them on lots split by the original developer into a housing court. They rented another of the small buildings as a shop and showroom. Josephine also began to acquire tiny corner lots, which she would unify into a single lot large enough to build a new two-story store and warehouse.

The Dejans continued to work hard, moving more and more furniture and saving what they could. This high-profile corner was close to the streetcars that ran down the median of Esplanade just a block away. The location guaranteed plenty of foot traffic from the daily commute of workers from colored communities of Tremé and Marigny to the rest of the city

Then, the South seceded and the war began.

＊

JEAN BENJAMIN

SON OF SIMEON ESNARD AND MARIE LOUISE SMITH

New Orleans, 1860

J EAN HAD JUST BEEN CONFIRMED AT ST. AUGUSTINE
Church when everything changed. He had heard the men arguing over
strong coffee in the sidewalk cafes all over the Quarter. They opined
about what a war would do to their business and to the security of the city.
The mere rumors of war had already slowed trade in many sectors, and cash
was growing tighter by the day. They depended on the money from the cotton
and sugar cane planters and the flow of fancy goods shipped from Europe to
feed the planters' desires. In both directions the men of the Quarter made
money off this trade. Many of them, white and free colored, had built for-
tunes on this ever-growing wave of commerce. But secession disturbed everything, and speculators who kept the cash flowing did not take kindly to the
uncertainty of war, which followed this audacious act of the South.

Jean watched from a distance as white men from the city marched off in
their gray-and-gold uniforms, with the fife and drum lending the cadence to
this noble defense of a fading lifestyle. Businessmen were up in arms because
the plantation trade had slowed so much and their inventories were growing
too large. It was spring, and a hint of summer heat threatened the still city,
the air rich with the scent of jasmine from the old courtyards.

Weeks later Jean learned from excited dockworkers that Union ships
were sailing upriver from the delta. The city, he learned, was protected just
downriver by a great chain barricade and four small batteries. Reports circu-
lated that while the Union was not faring well on the battlefield, their navy
was another matter. It was said they were supplied with many more ships
than the South, and their aim to blockade every port and strangle the Confederacy was not so far-fetched.

Major General Mansfield Lovell was commander of the Confederate River Defense Fleet, which included ten gunboats and the ironclads *Manassas* and *Louisiana*. On April 18, the Union's Admiral David Farragut began pounding the batteries with artillery, and they could hear it downtown in the Quarter where no one could sleep for the round-the-clock explosions.

On the fifth day of the conflict, Jean joined his friends to hike down the levee to see the impact of such a bombardment. They hid in the riverbank willows and listened to the cannons downriver, but they would not go closer, for the clouds of smoke rising just around the bend made it too dangerous. Then the firing slowed, and then it dwindled to an occasional explosion just as the stars and stripes appeared above the treetops.

The flag flew high atop Farragut's flagship. Its approach signaled to the Confederate ships anchored upriver to come down speedily with the current to ram the Union ships. Out front, ironclad *Manassas* began the terrible conflict. Jean Benjamin would never forget the flames and the screaming and the guns. The rest of Farragut's ships met the Confederate River Defense Fleet on April 24, the next day, and a battle ensued, one ship running aground, and in the chaos the *Manassas* found itself downstream of the Union ships. It was unable to turn around and power upriver again against the current, giving Farragut a clear shot at the city.

By the time Union ships dropped anchor on April 25, 1862, Jean Benjamin was there to see Farragut's officers enter the city. They requested General Lovell's surrender, but the man had retreated, leaving the city undefended. By the end of April the Union flag flew over an undamaged New Orleans, and the South would never be the same.

At home, Jean's father, Simeon, was ambivalent about the occupation. He was in full support of abolition and therefore supported the North, but occupation caused disruption in business. It would place great stress on his ability to support his enormous single-parent household. Fortunately the older children had reached an age to help out; some even found work to support the family. But while Simeon worried about his finances, he was also hopeful that the South would fall to the Union, granting him and his colored children new freedoms, above all, to leave town safely.

No one believed it would happen so soon and that the city would change hands so easily. Like all things during the war, the Confederates lacked the supply lines and mechanization of the North. Even their frigates and ironclads did not have nearly the firepower of the Northern ships, which also exceeded the South in numbers. Jean felt both fear and excitement at this turn of events. Change such as this led to a great deal of uncertainty, but as Simeon said, change could also result in great opportunity. None would understand that quite as much as the slave population eagerly anticipating their freedom.

Though the Confederate regiments fled the city, they did not invite the New Orleans regiments of the Louisiana Native Guards to join them. Instead they remained as a local militia, ostensibly to keep order, but the Union Army easily achieved that.

In those days before the war when the Confederate army was forming, the word had gone out that they wished to form a colored regiment. Simeon was not keen on letting any of his sons join what would be known as the Louisiana Home Guards. Many family meals had been spoiled by arguments between Simeon and his sons.

"You can't trust those men," he told them, his voice rising in pitch. "They do this strictly for political reasons. They'll never fight beside you under any circumstances."

"But, they promise to pay us well. And, *mon Dieu*, their uniforms are beautiful."

"Theo, a man is just as dead in a beautiful uniform as he is in rags. They tempt you with this, thinking we are as dull as the black men on their plantations. Don't rise to their bait like a catfish. Resist this because it's all for show. They've made so many similar promises and kept none of them. This war may put them down one day, but it'll never change them."

"Even if we fight for them and show our loyalty?"

"Lies. They will make you political pawns in the end. Remember, you're no different in their eyes from the slaves they buy and sell every day in this city. One step outside the city makes you one of them. If any of us fight, it should be for the North, for they have our best interests at heart."

Two of Jean's brothers defied their father and joined the new Southern regiment after admiring their neighbors in dashing uniforms, strutting up and down Canal Street. Gabrielle Simeon and Theophile would join the 1st Regiment of the Louisiana Native Guards Militia. The newspapers were filled with photos of those uniformed black men with captions noting how tolerant southerners were and that the black men did indeed have rights in the South.

Unknown to its members, the Native Guards were never officially mustered into the Confederate Army. Though charged with protecting the Quarter from the advancing Union Army, they did not have the power nor the orders to fight.

On the first of May, Captain Butler arrived in New Orleans and set up headquarters for the Union Army there. He was not well liked by the families of those fighting for the Confederacy, and the colored community was unsure how his presence would impact daily life.

"This is what I was afraid of," Simeon said one night when his sons had gathered to discuss Butler's influence. "Now you two Native Guards are in their gun sights. You made it obvious that you support the Confederacy, and now you're a part of it."

"Do you think the Union soldiers will come after us?" Theo asked nervously.

"You're part of the Confederate Army, so yes, I believe they will."

"Perhaps we should leave the city before they arrest us?"

"Outside New Orleans the slaves remain in bondage, and that means you are vulnerable too. Leave and you risk being arrested; stay here and you risk becoming a prisoner of war. It all depends on what Captain Butler decides to do with you impulsive Native Guards."

Butler knew the free colored class was a powerful tool in running the city, for they had the greatest stake in his success. They could be counted on to support him by gathering news through their links to the domestic workers who collected rumors and secrets behind closed doors in the homes of the wealthy.

Butler's first move was to gather the free colored men to himself. He mustered support of sympathetic Louisianans by creating his own 6th Regiment, largely composed of Irish immigrants. Within that regiment he'd create an all-colored division for those of African descent. It was named in June 1863 the 1st Corps de Afrique.

The Esnards gathered again on a hot June day to share gumbo with their father and discuss the news. "Now that Butler has created the 6th Regiment, I truly want to help him drive the Confederates into the sea," Simeon announced.

"You're not going to join, are you, Papa?"

Simeon smiled. "I'm not so old as you think, Theo. And I wish that history will see our family not as supporters of the slave trade but men who stood up to the old ways that kept us prisoners in this city. I have always dreamed of travel."

"But Papa," young Jean said. "You can't join alone. I'll go with you."

Gabrielle shook his head. "Not you, Jean. You're too young."

"But Papa will be in the same regiment with me."

"You should remain here and look after your sisters."

"No, I will go with Papa," Jean said, his fist pounding the table top in frustration.

"I've been thinking about this a long time," Gabrielle said. "Perhaps Theo and I made a mistake with the Native Guards, but perhaps we didn't. It all depends on who wins."

"And that determines how all of you, my strong sons, will live after the fight ceases. We may be completely freed or our lives will remain much the same as before. Remember, the war is far from over. At this point it's not clear who will prevail."

Theo added, "If the Confederates are successful, we are safe."

"No, Theo, only you and Gabrielle will be safe."

"But if the Union wins this horrible war, what then?"

"Then Jean and I will have to work that much harder to convince Captain Butler that you two are not traitors to the Union cause."

"Or," Theo said, drawing out his words, "we will have to convince General Lee that our father and younger brother aren't Union spies or sympathizers. That is, if you make it home alive."

Jean and Simeon both felt the need to become part of this new regiment. They both joined up, Jean becoming the drummer boy, pounding out the cadence when they marched. This division would travel throughout much of southern Louisiana gaining colored sympathizers along the way. They encountered no battles, and like the Confederate colored troops, they served largely as public relations forces.

But for Jean and Simeon it was the first time they had stepped outside the New Orleans city limits. Before the war they would be arrested and sold into slavery, so neither had seen any other part of Louisiana. It was surely a powerful education to encounter plantation life and see firsthand the lives of slaves who worked the cane fields.

But not all Louisianans appreciated their presence. Everywhere they went, the remnants of white families, mostly women and very old men, saw the black corps of the 6th Regiment as an insult heaped upon their losses. The very ascent of blacks in their social roles was degrading enough, but making them soldiers was deeply resented. Eventually those who had joined the Confederate Native Guards were assimilated into the 6th Regiment, but their early allegiance to the Confederacy would always stand as a mark against them.

Each day the New Orleans newspapers detailed staggering human losses on the battlefield time and again as Lincoln's frustration with his failed generals grew. There was much conflict in the Quarter as well. The *gens de couleur libres* sought common ground amid two warring governments, hoping that in the end they'd come out on the winning side.

When the war ended in the spring of 1865, Jean was considerably older and had learned much about the politics of race traveling with the Corps de Afrique. Jean obtained a much broader view of rural plantation life and the human chattel that kept it productive. Even the conflicts in his own family proved a foundation for his learning, and he began to read voraciously about the world outside of the South, where colored men enjoyed the same freedoms as whites. Daily newspapers reported devastation of the plantation system and what it could mean to the economy of the South. With its most vital commercial centers bombarded for weeks by merciless Union artillery, New Orleans remained miraculously unscathed.

Louisiana Confederates came home to find their city occupied by the Union Army, their bank accounts empty, and the free colored community faring quite well economically. Even more galling were the black men in Union uniforms who exacerbated the racial tensions among the older white families that had lost so much in the war. Their anger lay simmering just below the surface, ready to boil at a moment's notice. All that protected the Esnards from retribution was the Union Army.

To exploit the post-war opportunities, Northerners flooded into New Orleans to help rebuild the government of Louisiana and virtually every other Southern state. The new governments would be created from scratch, built excluding the old slave system to define the new rights and privileges for the former slaves. Following emancipation, many freed slaves, particularly those with some skills such as weaving or leatherwork, came into New Orleans to start their new life in the only place undamaged by the war. This pressured the former free colored community, who feared being lumped in with penniless men and women streaming in from the plantations. The free men of color feared that the old rigid caste system that granted them so many limited freedoms would vanish, causing them to lose status and be grouped in with illiterate slaves.

After the surrender of General Lee, Jean studied every issue of the colored newspaper, *New Orleans Tribune*. Driven by his father's fear that the old Confederate Democrats would manage to regain power in Louisiana, Jean saw many new opportunities arise in the effort to rebuild a new state government.

In order to put teeth into the Emancipation Proclamation, President Lincoln deemed that for a state to be readmitted to the Union, it must draft a new state constitution. In Washington they determined that Louisiana would become the first state to draft its new constitution, which could become a model for all other former slave-holding states. This process would

be done under close Union scrutiny to address the complex problem of defin-
ing and granting civil rights to a whole new group of people. Jean's fear shared
by the free colored community was that its emphasis would be too heavily
focused on slaves and deny sufficient attention to his community of free coloreds. This encouraged him to get involved in the process. He managed to get
himself appointed to the Constitutional Convention as a representative of
St. Mary's Parish, as Orleans was already well represented by wealthier, and
much older, free colored businessmen. He was barely twenty-one.

Jean Benjamin proudly joined the most accomplished free people of color
in Louisiana at the Cabildo in New Orleans, where the new constitution
was drawn up and drafted for the public in 1866. Its role was to legally and
clearly abolish slavery in every Louisiana parish and give full rights to black
men. That is, all rights except the vote, which had previously been limited
to landowning white males. To extend that right to virtually every former
illiterate male slave was too much to expect. But this was Jean's worst fear
embodied, that he and Simeon and all the merchants and craftsman of New
Orleans would have no opportunity to elect their own officials. They would
have no representation.

Jean, the youngest member of the Constitutional Convention, fought
day after day to gain the vote any way he could. In the end they conceded to
allow any colored man who fought for the Union to vote, which included Jean
and Simeon. It also divided those who had joined the Native Guards under
the Confederacy from those who enrolled in the Union Corps de Afrique.
Simeon had indeed been wise in advising his sons not to join the Native
Guards, and only he and Jean Benjamin would thus be allowed to vote. But
such a choice would lead to great conflict in the city, with riots and violence
on both sides threatening to tear its streets apart.

PART V

RECONSTRUCTION

❦

JOSEPHINE SCHAEFFER-KRACH-DEJAN

FRENCH IMMIGRANT WIFE OF PIERRE DEJAN

1869

JOSEPHINE AND PIERRE DEJAN STRUGGLED THROUGH the war years with their fledgling furniture business. The devastation upriver had all but eliminated demands for furniture in the rural areas. The Confederate families in the city were destitute as well. There was little cotton trade without slaves, leaving the city economically depressed. However, Josephine also saw opportunity. Many old wealthy families were forced to sell their homes and contents to get by. Many of these had collections of fine furniture, much of it imported from France. Never had Pierre seen such a market to buy excellent merchandise for pennies on the dollar.

At some point the Barracks and Dauphine corner became a two-story commercial building with its requisite decorative iron railings and tall windows opening onto the street. Madame Dejan Furniture remained profitable even during the war because they found new customers in the white speculators that came south to profit from misery there. These northerners had no concerns about coming to the colored merchants to do their business.

This map shows the French Quarter in 1869. On the right, where Dauphine and Barracks Streets meet, the dark rectangle shows the exact location of the Esnard-Dejan store and house.

Each day Pierre and Josephine kept track of the developing constitutional process. They knew it was key to their future, for as a white woman living with a colored man without the benefit of civil marriage, they felt legally vulnerable. The assets would,

by law, belong to the man, but because Pierre was colored, he was not protected by ordinary civil rights. Some whites were quite adept at fleecing coloreds both legally and illegally, which was why they tended to live and do
business within small neighborhoods of free coloreds like themselves, whom
they could trust.

There was always the chance that angry Confederates could look unfa-
vorably upon their cohabitation and question the legality of a marriage of
conscience. Without a marriage license, they had no protection in the courts.

Confederates who had returned from the war made it no secret that they
opposed the new constitution and its colored framers. Some former slaves
were incensed that they were denied the vote. Still more free coloreds who
enlisted with the Confederate armies were also denied the privilege. Above
all, the fear of former slaves running amok in civilized society frightened
both free coloreds and whites, so the Black Codes arose to set boundaries on
their social freedoms.

This raised tension in the city to palpable levels, and the colored community knew it was a fragile state of affairs. Already there had been violence
in the streets, with riots and fighting among black, colored, and white. The
current constitution would hold only so long as the Union Army protected
the conventioneers and office holders as well as quelled civil unrest on both
sides. Confederate Louisianans were not to remain quiet forever, and the
resentment boiled like an invisible pool of magma ready to blow the top off
a volcano.

Finally in 1868, a new version of the constitution was framed. Its goal
was to give full civil rights to all people of African ancestry both free and
slave. It also established cause for segregating former Confederates who
made it clear they would spend their lives fighting to return to their old way
of life. Many of these were wealthy white families entrenched in the government before the war. The problem was their tight connections with those in
the courts and law enforcement.

The moment the new constitution went into effect, interracial marriage became legal. Pierre and Josephine sought to legally ratify their 1858
marriage of conscience. It would not do to simply marry immediately under
the new law, for that would only protect them from that day forward. They
required the marriage to fully recognize their first union. That would ensure
retroactive protections as well.

In February 1869, Pierre and Josephine were remarried in the Second
Justice's Court by Judge John P. Montamat. This not only bound their joint
assets into one estate, but they could also finally stand proud in public

without fear that their illegal union would be discovered. It was a great day for both of them, and many others of similar estate were also legalizing their unions as quickly as possible.

During Reconstruction there was much talk of the Union Army eventually returning to the North. Louisiana had to regain self-rule at some point, and Confederates were counting the days. Everyone in the Quarter knew that without military strength as a foundation for their newly won civil rights, they could not count on those newfound freedoms remaining sound. Pierre and Josephine understood the transient nature of this period of new freedoms. They also knew that New Orleans could revert to its former segregated status overnight. The Confederates had organized themselves into the Democratic Party and lobbied heavily using their powers and contacts in Washington to put pressure on the administration to remove the army from Louisiana.

The Dejans knew there would be trouble when that day came. As one of the rare marriages of a colored man and white woman, they could be torn apart in the courts and their assets seized. Already the planters were working to lure hungry former slaves back to the farms to labor for bed and board or, worse, as sharecroppers on worn-out cotton land. Wages in the city were too low for freed slaves to survive, with jobs for unskilled labor few and far between. This forced many without education or enough money back to plantation life. A new form of slavery was being established in Louisiana.

With such prospects looming just over the horizon, Pierre and Josephine took another bold step to protect their growing assets. As a white woman, Josephine would enjoy full civil rights. Laws on community property in Louisiana kept family assets in the husband's name. They knew there was only one way to solve the problem of Pierre's vulnerability as a colored man—and that was to put it all in Josephine's name. This was not easy to do because it required a legal judgment, and with the end of Reconstruction looming, every mixed-race family in New Orleans sought to protect their savings and investments by transferring them into the ownership of the whitest members. But rarely was this spouse a white woman, however, so the Dejan's transfer would be particularly difficult.

Their strategy was to state that at the time of their 1858 marriage of conscience, Madame Dejan brought $28,000 with her into that union. Therefore, that was not community property but her sole and separate wealth.

Just four months after their February 1868 civil marriage, Josephine and Pierre again went to the city of New Orleans. There they filed a will for Mrs. Dejan, which would be used to establish exactly what she owned at the time of the ratification. It stated that at the time of her first marriage she came to that union with $28,000 of her own money obtained "by her industry and through happy circumstances." This amount is coincidentally the total this couple owned together at the time of this 1869 filing. What the will did was simply establish it as her own assets. To make it look better, she bequeathed $10,000 to her husband and the remainder to her two daughters, Florentine and Pauline, whom she left behind in France as babies. She also indicated Pierre as the executor of that will upon her death.

The legal marriage and the declaration of her sole and separate property from roughly fifteen years before would protect them legally should the tone of Louisiana government turn against colored members of the family.

Now the Dejans were legal in the eyes of the state and the church. Many years had passed since Josephine had seen her daughters, and they had grown up into mature young women. Josephine had no way to know how they felt about being summoned to New Orleans, but now that the war was over, the new constitution protected them and she was legally married, and she felt it was safe enough to bring her daughters from France.

Florentine Krach was about eighteen years old when she sailed for Louisiana with her younger sister, Pauline.

The girls arrived in 1871 with their trunks and boxes, finding the new city completely different from that of their cool, green homeland. Here was a city that simmered in the sweltering heat, and terrible political pressures threatened to boil over daily. The daughters did not move in with the Dejans but rented a small house nearby. Suddenly they would come to know the mother who had immigrated so long ago, and no doubt there were questions that would be difficult to answer. Why did you leave us so young? Why didn't you come back when you found out Papa was dead? Why did it take so long to send for us?

Nobody knows for sure how they fared reuniting, but it is clear that the girls came to know their stepfather quite well. Years later Pauline would name him godfather for one of her children. Being French and speaking no English, they settled easily into life in the Quarter, but they did not share the same bias as white Americans. They would soon be employed at Madame Dejan Furniture—where the two young girls certainly did not hurt sales.

FLORENTINE KRACH
ELDEST DAUGHTER OF JOSEPHINE SCHAEFFER-KRACH-DEJAN
AND PAUL KRACH

New Orleans, 1871

FLORENTINE KRACH BOTH LOVED AND HATED HER mother. She longed for the woman who bore her but deeply resented the fact that she had abandoned them. Certainly there were political problems—that she knew—but for over fifteen years Josephine did little more than send money for her schooling and an occasional letter. Those written words from America were from a woman she didn't know.

Change was difficult for Florentine, who had lived so many years in highly organized convent schools. She was suddenly thrust into the metropolitan New Orleans with its legendary waterfront, prostitution, and smuggling. The humid Louisiana climate would leave her stifled in her corset during the summer months, growing vapid under the least amount of physical exertion. Her little sister, Pauline, was even more miserable and complained unceasingly. She threatened at least once a week to return home as soon as she could save enough for her passage. Nothing in the new city appealed to her, and with the open sewers, cockroaches, rain, and sweating walls, she was repulsed by it all.

Then it all changed for Florentine when Monsieur Esnard came into the shop. He was there to pick up a check for his father's work on a set of chairs delivered the week before. They were made of bald cypress, designed to match an old French parquetry table that Pierre had picked up for a song at auction. It had come out of the only building still standing at a sugarcane plantation in the delta. Had it been anything but bald cypress, the table would have long ago rotted away. When Pierre first sanded down the surface mottled with fungus and mildew, its beautiful grain proved beyond comparison. Mama Dejan took one look at the new surface and dictated that she would go to Simeon to have eight chairs made to match it. Together they would make a healthy profit.

At her request, Simeon had come over to take a look at the table and peruse Dejan's catalogs of the latest European chair designs. His calloused fingers and cracked nails seemed out of place in the spotless showroom turning one snow-white page after the next, nodding his head and occasionally offering a whispered word of praise.

"I recommend the chairs have upholstered seats," he said finally.

"Perhaps deep blue silk dotted with gold," Madame Dejan remarked, already thinking the same thing as she cradled a thick booklet of sample upholstery fabrics. "That would appeal both to the Americans and the old French. They both share weakness for dark blue and gold." She held up one sample for him to see.

"It is perfection. I am on my way. *Adieu*, Madame."

Simeon always agreed with Madame's way with style, which explained why she and Pierre had been so successful. When they finally assembled the whole set in the front window of Madame's store, Florentine helped dress it with a silver pitcher and cut-glass wine goblets. It was elegant and stylish. Everyone who passed by the window stopped to admire this seemingly new table and the elegantly upholstered chairs.

That day when Simeon sent his son Jean to pick up a check from the Dejans, Florentine saw him through the window. It was a small errand for a man in the legislature, so well dressed in a finely tailored suit and emerald silk vest accented with a shiny gold watch chain.

Compared to his wizened father, Jean was a large, charismatic, and handsome man with straight black hair and bristly mustache that obscured his mouth. He would wear this feature throughout his life, even into old age, perhaps to prevent a view of his overly full lips, a sensual characteristic that would define many future generations of the family.

Florentine returned from lunch to find the well-dressed man inside admiring the table. He appeared to be a potential customer for this expensive set. Mama Dejan appeared from the depths of the store and handed him an envelope, which he slid into his inside pocket. Then he smiled, his somber dark face lighting up to reveal a set of perfect white teeth beneath the edges of the mustache. His charm overflowed, and Florentine knew immediately this man was a force.

Her eyes did not leave Jean for a minute as he chatted with her mother. Florentine remained quiet, distractedly dusting the other pieces of furniture while she listened in as Josephine discussed local politics with the well-spoken fellow.

"Monsieur Esnard, I am concerned that the Union Army is preparing to vacate the city. Have you heard anything that would validate their departure? Naturally Pierre is quite concerned."

"It will be soon, Madame. Perhaps at the end of the year."

"And then what?"

"That's anyone's guess. I do suspect they will do their best to oust all of us when election time comes 'round."

"And if you lose your seat, then things may return to the way they were before the war."

"There is no way to know, but Lincoln's Emancipation Proclamation cannot be undone, so even if they do away with the new constitution, they cannot return those men and women to slavery."

"But there are other ways to hurt us."

"Oh yes, and many of them could hurt us because once the balance of power changes in the statehouse, they fill our offices with disgruntled veterans who have only one desire: to return to the old ways."

"How quickly will this change come?"

"It depends on the outcome of elections. I would think it will change slowly bit by bit. They will override the constitution with one small law at a time so it remains unnoticed outside our state. They don't want to raise concerns in Washington, but there's no question they'll use the courts in every way they can. They are patient and tenacious. Dripping water can wear away stone, and they will never give up."

After that day, Jean came often to the Dauphine Street corner to bring Mama Dejan the news. Soon Florentine was absorbing all the news too, then asking intelligent questions of Monsieur Esnard. Mama Dejan initially failed to notice her daughter's sidelong glances, but in time she realized the two were sharing far more than a discussion of local politics.

One day Florentine walked Jean out to the banquette, then joined him in further discussion before finally returning to the store.

"*Mon Dieu*, what are you doing, Florentine? That man is not for you." Mama Dejan's face showed marked disapproval, her lips thin and tight.

"Is it because he too is colored, like Pierre?"

Mama Dejan relaxed into a lounge chair and brushed gray hairs out of her eyes, a look of exasperation in her face.

"The problem is not that he's colored, for he was born here and cannot change that. But for you, a white woman, things will be different. His presence can become a real threat to your life once the Union Army goes home. And if things go back to the way they were, you may not be able to marry at all. My dear, it will drag you down no matter how much you love him. Don't white men interest you?"

Florentine's face grew hard. "It's because of you, Mother, that I am in this position. You chose to marry Pierre, not once but twice! He is a colored man and very well known. Who would marry a girl whose stepfather is colored? "

Tears came to Josephine's eyes as she stood and turned to her oldest daughter.

"Forgive me. I did not mean for you to live in this shadow of my love for Pierre."

Florentine softened, taking her mother in her arms. "I understand, Maman, that life has never been easy for you. At home we had so many more men to choose from, but here in New Orleans, the only white men who won't care about Pierre are the immigrants, and they are poor and uneducated. At least Jean is a man who knows how the world turns."

"There will be no denying his past, daughter. His family is too well known here for you to live quietly as I have with Pierre. You won't be able to hide this truth in New Orleans. You realize change will come and so do I. My lawyer says this may prove the worst time possible to become involved with this man no matter how successful he is."

"Maman, let me ask you one question. Why did you marry Pierre?"

"Because I loved him, of course."

"Then should I fall in love with Jean, you can't expect me to walk away."

"Yes, that's true. But think about your children if you are lucky enough to bear them. God did not bless me with children with Pierre, so we don't have to cross that bridge." Mama Dejan's lip quivered however slightly, and Florentine had come to recognize it as one of the few clues to what was really in her heart. "Perhaps it is a blessing," she added in a half whisper. "Pierre has told me of his sadness at not being part of my white world, nor did he wholly exist in the black one. That will be the fate or your children with Jean Benjamin Esnard."

————— ⚜ —————

JEAN BENJAMIN

FATHER OF A DYNASTY

New Orleans, 1874

J EAN LOVED HIS LIFE AS A BACHELOR POLITICIAN. WHEN the legislature was not in session, he hunted the bayous, played chess in the cafes, enjoyed a bottle of wine when he pleased, and relished the great food that made his city famous. Yet he found himself spending more and more time with Florentine Krach, the daughter of the furniture dealer. Her mother's displeasure was obvious, but they were white and Jean was used to it. Florentine just shrugged it off and seemed to enjoy his presence as he introduced her to so many people throughout the Quarter. Everyone seemed to know and love Jean, and Florentine looked forward to his visits.

Jean knew it was a rare thing to find a white woman so out of touch with racial politics. She was indeed willing to love a colored man; though, if a person met him for the first time, he would indeed pass for white. He hoped she would marry him, not only because he loved her, but also because a white wife would aid him greatly in politics. He knew political change was in the winds and what might happen should the Democrats return to power. They could indeed undo much of the Constitution and make it illegal once again to marry a person of color. He did not want that to happen before they were legally married. Jean would never ask Florentine to live under a marriage of conscience as her mother did, for as a white woman she deserved more than that. They all deserved more than that.

Pauline finally had enough of New Orleans and demanded to be sent back home. She had no interests whatsoever in spending the rest of her life in the Quarter, particularly since Florentine was now with Jean much of the time. Pauline was lonely. She argued with her mother and stepfather incessantly, causing tensions to rise at the store. Jean knew of Pauline's dissatisfaction with her new home and grew fearful that she'd convince Florentine to go home with her. If Flo left even for a short time, there was no guarantee she'd ever come back. So Pauline left.

There was no church wedding. Jean and Florentine went directly to Mama Dejan's lawyer, Judge Theard, and were married in a civil ceremony. This sound, legal action was to ensure the union would never be questioned in the courts. Civil marriage could never be confused with a prior marriage of conscience. They moved into Jean's apartment, a bittersweet beginning, for their world began to change suddenly, and all too soon.

The national presidential election of 1877 ended in a stalemate. An enormous dispute ensued as to which man would occupy the White House: Democrat Samuel J. Tilden or Jean's man, Republican Rutherford B. Hayes. The conflict was so great that many feared another civil war would break out between the North and South. The war-weary Federals sought to reconcile the two parties any way they could.

In a convoluted negotiation process that was largely undocumented and finalized just days before the inauguration, southern Democrats agreed to support Hayes only if the stranglehold of the Union Army was removed from Louisiana, South Carolina, and Florida. This outcome justified Jean's worst fears.

The Confederates had moved their cause to Washington in a strategy to end Reconstruction by exerting pressure on the Union Army to leave New Orleans. The long-standing links to Washington political machines were used effectively to put candidates against the Republicans, who were largely poor whites, uneducated blacks, and the rising colored class. The agreement involved four terms, but only one was ever enacted: the removal of federal troops from the South. It was done immediately, with crushing consequences. The door was now open for Southern Democrats to crank up their political machine and redeem their government.

With the Union Army gone, the climate of New Orleans was changing. Though it had always been a raucous city, the incidents of violence were growing exponentially. Jean Benjamin and other legislators were trying desperately to keep up with the changes both in Washington and at home. White groups were forming in the city to intimidate blacks and coloreds. Jean was concerned his family may be threatened to force him to step down. It had happened to other colored men in the legislature, and with his family's unusual racial marriages involving white women, they were doubly at risk.

The strategy was to discourage blacks from voting so that whites would constitute more of the electorate. This involved intimidation tactics designed to frighten poor and illiterate voters, particularly in the rural areas. Armies of night riders spread out to remind blacks to remain at home on Election Day or face the consequences.

One by one the Democrats ran their white candidates against blacks who had been in office since the end of the war. The incumbents had no way to mount defensive campaigns. Democrats had enough time since Lee's surrender to fill their new political war chests. Jean could feel his security slipping away. The death knell was a new federal regulation stating that Southern police forces need not prosecute violent whites for racially motivated crimes if the state that employed them chose not to. Without federal intervention the growing colored class could not defend themselves in the streets, in the voting booth, or in court.

More than once Jean Benjamin Esnard thought he would walk away from his office out of fear for his family. It was Simeon who talked him into staying for the sake of the rights that he had fought so hard to establish. "You can't walk out on your people, Jean," the old man said. "If you ever ran for office again, they'd never vote for you. They need you to be loyal to the end, no matter what it costs." But Simeon was old and Jean knew the score. It was only a matter of time for a colored man married to a white woman to become suspect. In the not-too-distant future, that same government would consider such a marriage as little more than rape.

PART VI

DEJAN V. DEJAN

MAMA DEJAN

MATRIARCH

New Orleans, 1877

THE USED FURNITURE BUSINESS EXPLODED DUE TO THE plethora of fine furnishings coming downriver to sell in New Orleans. Furniture was among the few items the Yankees could not carry away with them, and it was the last bit of value remaining in these formerly lavish homes. Pierre was busy at every auction picking up more inventory, knowing it would fetch ten times what he paid at the store.

The Dejan coffers were filling, and Josephine often consulted with Pierre on the state of affairs over French wine in the evenings, when the store was closed and they could be alone together.

"At the auction today, before bidding started, I overheard some white men in front of me speaking openly about the situation at the statehouse."

"There's nothing we can do about the way it's going, Pierre. It's in God's hands, and I'm praying every day that he will protect us. The same old families who ran this city before the war now have their sons and grandsons doing their bidding."

"My concern is that they may see our union as immoral."

"But it's legal."

"Legal so far, but those men also said they were making every effort to outlaw marriage between whites and our people. If our marriage is deemed illegal, I'm afraid they will come for my half of our assets. The way things are going, it looks risky to challenge them because they now control the police and the statehouse. We have no one to turn to for help."

"I spoke with Mr. Theard last week, and he advised me to divide the assets as we did eight years ago. That way all our money is deemed my sole and separate property. They won't come after you for money if nothing is in your name."

72

"Too many families we know have done the same thing, and the bureaucrats are quite aware of that strategy. Mr. Theard will have to find another solution for us that won't bring so much scrutiny to our activities."

Pierre filled his wife's crystal goblet with burgundy. "I've given it some thought, and we have one option, but only if you approve."

Josephine took a sip and then dabbed her lips with a handkerchief. "So what do you propose?"

"My dear, your safety and that of our family is more important than my reputation, is it not?"

"Yes, but where are you going with this?"

"Before he died, my papa told me and my brothers to never trust the banks. We both know that, and it's why we invest our money so it can never be stolen. Accounts of colored men and women who can no longer defend themselves in the courts will be the first to vanish. So imagine this, my dear. If I was deemed irresponsible, say I drank too much and gambled away your money, then the court would protect you by allowing our accounts to become yours exclusively."

"Oh, but I could never make such claims! You're an honorable man, Pierre. Everyone knows that."

"Our friends and acquaintances do, but not the courts." Pierre winked, then gave a wry smile as he said, "I will gladly give you my share of our community property in order to keep you safe from my vices."

"I could never ask you to surrender your reputation just to keep our money safe."

"The truth is, I'm an old colored man, so my reputation is not so important compared to the security we could gain in the end."

Josephine blinked back tears as she realized just how much Pierre was willing to sacrifice. "I will visit Theard tomorrow, then, and share with him your proposal."

Theard was in his office the following day as Josephine stepped out of a cab onto the banquette. She arranged her voluminous skirts and entered the building where the family lawyer kept his offices on the ground floor.

"Ah, Madame Dejan, what can I do for you today?" Theard said, standing behind his broad desk littered with papers and thick law books.

Josephine sat before him and repeated Pierre's offer.

When she had finished, Theard leaned back in his chair, the springs squeaking quietly. "You are fortunate, Madame, to have married such a selfless man. Few would make such a sacrifice for the good of a family. In order to put this plan into action, we have much work to do for it to appear convincing to the court. There must be proof."

"Proof of Pierre's debts?"

"Exactly. Suppose the creditors sent letters to prove his default."

"But we have no creditors."

"To be sure. I suspect Jean Benjamin will help you find trustworthy associates willing to become temporary creditors. Perhaps a stipend would encourage their participation. They would become natural witnesses to the fact. We must draw up a note for each one, then you must obtain a receipt that states you paid it off. This would then turn all moneys paid into a single large debt, proving Pierre owes you that money paid to the creditors. It is a complicated solution, but this way it will pass through the court properly."

"It will take time, you know. To set up the debts."

"Then we'd better start now. Anyone willing to sacrifice his good name for the financial welfare of the family is an honorable man. Let's hope he remains that way."

Mama Dejan's efforts to keep her money in investments rather than cash resulted in a sizable estate. She had purchased many buildings in the Quarter, renting out the storefronts, apartments, and rooms for a healthy monthly income. With many well-to-do colored merchants unable or simply afraid of banking under the changing government, Mama Dejan had made interest-bearing loans with notes duly filed and legal. Their additional savings as well as their expanding inventory now amounted to a great deal, and the same old fears of losing it all returned.

Everyone in New Orleans sensed the great shift of power. Recent violence and uncertainty made the colored community uneasy with the change. The registrar's office was flooded with requests for changes of ownership, marriages, and other methods of shifting wealth to more protected status. Many of these were being routinely denied because it was obvious what was going on. These machinations had no other purpose than to position for security.

So Pierre's name began to appear on debts related to the store. They were sizeable, and it is very likely that Mama Dejan had previous conversations with the creditors. Pierre's name would be on these bills and he would default, creating a paper trail of collection efforts.

Once the debts had been sufficiently documented, Mama Dejan hired another attorney not associated with her earlier suit. Attorney J. Tharp would sue Pierre to have his share of their joint moneys put in her control. This would make her the sole manager and administrator in perpetuity. All went as Theard had predicted. She won the suit, putting it all—money, real estate, notes, and inventory—in her name. The business itself would bear her name only: Madame Dejan Furniture. Of course nothing changed dramatically within the family or the store. Pierre still attended the auctions and collected rents. Madame Dejan hired Pierre's brother, Jules Dejan Jr., to keep the books throughout the entire process.

After the end of Reconstruction, the climate in New Orleans shifted from an all-inclusive government to one that sought to reduce the number of colored office holders and their voting blocks. The White League and the Knights of the White Camellia formed to intimidate freed slaves from seeking the vote. Seat by seat was vacated by its former colored official and claimed by Southern Democrats who immediately set about framing amendments to the new constitution. All colored families in New Orleans stepped up their efforts to protect themselves as Mama Dejan had.

A little over a year after Raoul, her first, was born, Florentine gave birth to her second son, Paul Filbert. They called Doctor Degas, just as Jean had with his first son, to ensure that the birth record was properly filled out. He hoped to make certain that none of his children would ever bear that horrible C that could doom them all.

St. Augustine's would become the family church for both the Dejans and Esnards. It was built just before the Civil War by a mixture of white and colored residents from the area who donated their money to finish it. Land in the new Tremé farbourg was less expensive than Marigny, and it would serve the colored community of both neighborhoods. The Esnards no doubt participated in the race of the pews, where white and coloreds competed to donate the most pews. The colored community was more organized at the time and purchased twice as many for themselves, thereby laying claim to the church as one never to be segregated. This church would count Homer Plessy among its parishioners. The old Tremé family home that stood on the church property was used as a school for young black girls by Henriette Delille, a colored Catholic nun.

Adrienne was born in 1877, the first daughter of Jean and Florentine. With so many babies to care for, Florentine was always home now and her husband became

St. Augustine Church is located in Tremé not far from the Esnard home. It would become the center of religious life for this Catholic family and many other important figures in early civil rights struggles in that city.

clerk and salesman for Mama Dejan with a brief stint as lottery agent. Florentine also kept the cash for the store at her home, where it was easily accessible. Mama Dejan kept an account at Canal Bank, but it was merely for holding funds briefly during the process of a large purchase or payment. Most of the time it sat nearly empty with just a few dollars on account until a family member deposited the cash and immediately withdrew it as a cashier's check to complete the transaction.

None of them trusted the bank despite their bookkeeper, Jules Dejan Jr., and his efforts to encourage them to deposit in the Citizens Bank managed by his father. Though laws changed little in the first years after the Union Army vacated the city, it seemed as if they all were simply holding their breath, waiting for the inevitable oppression to come.

What Jean did notice was a return of the haughtiness of whites toward the colored class, now far more arrogant than they had ever been before the war. In the early days they all knew their place but treated each other with formality and respect, for there was little threat to either side. But since the war ripped these older moral codes to shreds, and cumulative white anger over the loss of their lifestyle grew, none of that original *détente* survived.

This portrait of Adrienne Esnard taken in New Orleans shows her natural beauty early in life. She and her equally beautiful sisters Flo and Jo did not marry nor did they have children, which is very unusual in a devout Catholic family

Jean Benjamin was a target because he had been a politician during Reconstruction. There was no way around that. To avoid potential conflict, Jean skirted white neighborhoods and society, sending his hired man to make deliveries where he would too easily be recognized. A new set of unwritten laws was taking over the city, ones that made any contact of colored men with whites a losing proposition. What galled him the most about these subtle constraints was the fact that the white man now, no matter how ignorant, was always right. Even a man of Jean's standing could not contradict a white man, and should he do so, or God forbid he should fight back if attacked by one, he would be immediately jailed. With yet another child on the way, none of them could take that risk anymore.

PIERRE DEJAN

New Orleans, 1885

P IERRE HAD FELT THE PAIN GROWING, BUT HE DID NOT
mention it to his wife, Josephine. Any sign of discomfort found her flut-
tering around him like a nurse, making sure he was comfortable and well
fed. She doted on him, and without children they were unusually close. Now
that their assets were safely under her name, they could move ahead with
plans for a new house. It would be built where their tiny cottage now stood
next to the store. It would be a beautiful French man-sard roof townhouse like those in the finer parts of town. Josephine desired to show their success with this home, and it would be the most elegant one in the neighborhood.

Over the past years, Josephine had carefully acquired all six of the tiny lots formerly known as the Pillie subdivision. The former owner, Jacques Zino, had split a much larger piece of property in 1793, and Pillie, the sur-veyor, created the group

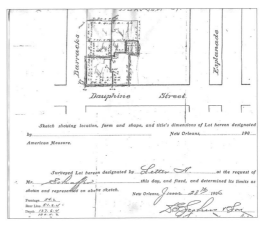

This survey taken in 1906 shows the corner of Dauphine and Barracks with its warren of tiny lots created in the eighteenth century. This is where Pierre Dejan's cottage stood, the house he and Mama Dejan lived in after their Catholic marriage of conscience in 1856 when it was illegal for races to intermarry. Mama Dejan would buy up all of the lots in order to build the store on the corner and later the house next door. This survey likely helped to prepare the property for resale when the Esnards were putting their affairs in order to relocate to Los Angeles.

of small lots for individual homes to be built on. Likely these were either to be rentals or speculation homes to be sold at a considerable profit. They would be known as Creole cottages, and this was a popular way to develop real estate that would offset the cost of laying out larger subdivisions.

Pierre and Josephine had talked many nights about a new house with indoor plumbing and gas lights. Madame Dejan filed for building permits, which were approved to begin work in September 1885. Business was suspended once the demolition was done, and both Josephine and Pierre were anxious to keep construction moving so life would return to normal as quickly as possible. They were no longer young, and the upheaval was exhausting.

Of course it took more time than they expected, which was a strain on both the Dejans. Finally they were able to move in during the summer of 1886, the home crisp and clean with rooms filled with light. The Esnard children ran up and down the stairs as workmen brought in their new furniture from the store.

Perhaps it was the strain of building the house or the growing concern over political change that caused the pain. It did not keep him from taking coffee with his friends down the street, but it was too difficult for Pierre to attend the auction, so Jean and his oldest son, Raoul, went for him. They all noticed that Pierre had slowed down, but the store was now quite successful as their assets and financial security grew steadily under his wife's management and Jean Benjamin's excellent mind for investments. Pierre liked to sit among Florentine's children and tell them stories of his own childhood in the old city before the war. Their newest sibling, Rene, was nearly two years old now, a bright and social child who came to love his *grand-père*, delighting every time the old man pulled his engraved gold watch from his vest to hear it chime.

Florentine loved Pierre dearly. In those first years after she had come to America, he had created a special relationship with her sister, Pauline, listening patiently to her misery and complaints about Louisiana and pleading to go back home to Alsace. Pierre had even set aside money for her return voyage, for he knew she would never find a home in his world. She was too European and had too great a link to the Schaeffer relatives who had raised her.

It was not long until the pain began to climb into his chest, which forced Pierre to remain at home while Mama Dejan tended the store. He missed his old friends and the daily coffee when they would chat for hours about the many new laws and regulations. They often discussed the growing number of "Whites Only" signs that had been posted in some businesses owned by former Confederates around the outer edges of the Quarter. At least most of the old city remained strongly colored.

Pierre often pondered why they again found themselves sequestered in the old city, not by fear of slavery but by the many legal limitations on where they could go to eat and drink. What made it all so frightening was that the police were clearly unwilling or unable to help them should an infraction occur. He bristled at seeing every one of these "whites only" edicts posted clearly in places he had often frequented before the war. Now he had to comply with the signs: "Coloreds enter at rear." "Colored restroom." Even the schools were splitting into black and white. As a colored family, Florentine's children were forced to leave their school to attend another one, a private institution. She immediately enrolled them into St. Augustine's parochial school. Pierre saw the exclusions appearing everywhere, subtle yet powerfully designed to keep him and his people ensconced in their neighborhoods.

It was just before the Feast of All Souls in 1886 that Josephine woke to find Pierre had died peacefully in his sleep. There he lay in their large carved bedstead in the bright new room. His normally caramel-colored face had grown ashy white and cold, and her tears fell upon the sheets as she sat beside him remembering their life together. Twenty-seven years, two marriages, and decades of beautiful furniture had bound them together through the most turbulent times in the history of America. He had cared for her daughters like his own. He had become the adoring grand-père of Florentine's brood. Pierre had even become godfather by proxy of one of Pauline's children in Rheims.

Through it all he had remained loving, hardworking, and dedicated to her, allowing her to use her substantial intelligence in an era when women rarely held their own assets or ran businesses. She knew she had not been a perfect wife, perhaps too stern and driven, but her memory of life in France and those early years at the Schmidt house haunted her with nightmares of grinding poverty and servitude.

Pierre had shared his small inheritance with her, the money distributed by his uncle to help them buy property. He had worked side by side with her, stripping and varnishing, cleaning and carrying piece by piece, making them both experts on fine French woodwork in their own right.

In this quiet moment, she lamented most of all that she had not been able to give him children. She had suffered miscarriages. Each time it was just a few months before the bleeding began. Florentine's babies became so precious that both he and Josephine doted on every one. And she knew that little Rene would miss Pierre most of all, which caused her tears to flow.

Soon everyone knew that Pierre Dejan had passed. His brother Victor had helped them set up a viewing of the body in the house, with everyone thankful it had cooled off enough to make that possible. The funeral was massive, filling all of St. Augustine. Father Subileau said the funeral mass and rosary. Most of their friends, relatives, and neighbors joined the procession to the graveyard behind the gilded hearse drawn by two black horses. A group of Pierre's friends played their horns in a sad dirge as they walked, everyone draped in mourning. Josephine followed the priest, flanked by Florentine and Jean Benjamin. Behind them the children followed in their darkest Sunday clothes tended by one of Jean's sisters, who also managed her own children as well. Among them were Pierre's three brothers, Jules Jr., Victor, and Antoine.

Every table in the new house was crowded with flowers and dishes of food to feed the many Esnard mouths during those difficult days after losing Grand-père. Josephine prayed for strength and thanked God often for allowing him to live until the house was completed so they would have a short time together there. God had blessed her with success, but just as it reached its greatest peak, he had taken Pierre, in a reminder that all things are fleeting in this world and that despite her financial success, the loss of her love put it all in perspective.

In the months after Pierre died, Josephine, wrapped in widow's weeds, threw herself into work, buying inventory for the store and directing her workmen. Pierre was gone, and Josephine felt that with him went her own past. She embraced a future focused solely on taking care of her daughter's family as best she could, knowing the racial stranglehold was tightening into what would become known as the era of Jim Crow.

JULES DEJAN JR.

New Orleans, 1887

THE MONEY JULES DEJAN HAD SET UP FOR HIS ILLEGITI-mate sons had long been used up. While their white father rested in one cemetery, their mother was buried in a separate graveyard for col-oreds. When Pierre died, Jules Jr. was keeping the books for Mama Dejan's store and knew all too well the details of their business. He was fully aware of how much was earned by Madame Dejan Furniture and her many other investments.

The three surviving Dejan brothers sat at Du Monde drinking coffee when the matter came up. "She should share it with us," Victor said angrily. "After all, he was our brother—our natural brother. Doesn't the law say that inheritance should be shared among brothers?"

Jules corrected him. "Papa said that does not apply if there is a surviving spouse. Madame Josephine is his wife, and everything now belongs to her."

"But what if they were not legally married?"

Jules paused, absorbing what his brother had said. "The 1858 marriage of conscience was not legal, I grant you that. However, I testified in the suit in 1867 that she had twenty-eight thousand of her own money. That is just as Pierre asked me to. How can I now go back on that and say it was his?"

"The 1869 marriage will not be valid either," Victor added. "Democrats in the statehouse are already talking about those Reconstruction marriages as being shams."

Antoine added, "It was illegal from the start. Ratifying it, even ten years later, doesn't make it legal."

"May I remind you, little brother," Jules admonished him, "we are not white. They will find in her favor, always."

"And we are not legitimate either," Victor said softly after slowly sipping the demitasse. "So in the eyes of the law, we aren't legally related to Pierre."

"Her daughters will inherit all of it, both Josephine and Pierre's shares." Jules added. "According to what I've seen, it would be at least a hundred thousand dollars according to their books. A considerable sum, to be sure."

It was clear by their surprise that Antoine and Victor had no idea the fortune had grown to such a figure.

"There must be some way to prove that the marriages aren't valid, Jules. Perhaps we should discuss it with a lawyer. Papa would have. He had very unusual ways of getting around things like this, and he always used the lawyer."

Jules looked away at the busy traffic, horses clattering over the cobblestones. "I understand the Labatt brothers have done well with succession cases."

"It can be of no harm to inquire."

"Perhaps not to you, Antoine. But Madame Dejan is my client, and if she learns I'm plotting against her, there is no question I will be fired. Though I was never fond of the woman, she does pay my wages on time. And if I challenge her and, worse even, reveal her finances to the public courts, I will lose many other clients in her circle of merchants too. You, my brothers, have nothing to lose."

"Oh, but Jules, it's one hundred thousand dollars! Just imagine fifty thousand split three ways."

Jules gave it some thought and finally paid a call to Monsieur Labatt for a discussion of the matter. He was surprised to find the attorney far younger than expected, and it was clear he had newly joined the bar. His smallish office was on a side street that did not suggest great prosperity. After the man patiently listened to Jules lay out their situation, he perked up when Jules explained how much money was at risk.

Jules and his brothers returned the next day for a longer meeting. By then Monsieur Labatt had grown so enthusiastic he agreed to take the case on contingency. "A Louisiana law of 1844 says that if there are no heirs of the union, as is the case with Dejans, then the total estate is to be divided with half granted to relatives of the decedent, which would be you gentlemen. However, this is only true if there are questions of the validity of the marriage."

"So it is fertile ground to attack Pierre's marriage, or should I say marriage of conscience and ratification? If we can prove it is illegal, would his share be unquestionably ours?" Jules asked.

"That's our best strategy," the lawyer replied. "We must also show the woman is of low moral standing in her efforts to keep all the assets in her name. The fact that you, Jules, have kept Madame Dejan's books gives us an inside view of their estate. You would be the best witness of all."

Victor, ever the pragmatic brother, asked, "But you know as we do that she is white and so are the courts. With the way things are today, do we have a chance of winning?"

"Oh, but her marriage can work in our favor too. She's a woman who would live and, dare I say, marry a colored man. That suggests a woman of low standards in the eyes of many in this city. Add that to any deception discovered in her business dealings, she will not present good character to the court."

"And you will bring the suit simply on contingency?"

"Fifty thousand dollars is a good deal of money. This case may set an entirely new precedent. The judges are not so inclined to find in favor of whites that are in sympathy with coloreds."

"With our people?" Victor asked.

"Yes, with your *gens de couleur libres*. So if we pursue this, gentlemen, we must strive to keep your family out of the picture except for the relationship between you brothers."

"So we would be inspected too?"

"I'm afraid so, but I'll try to prevent that any way I can. As illegitimate sons, it can be argued that you are not entitled to a single thing. That is the biggest hurdle for us."

Soon after the Dejan brothers appeared before Monsieur Labatt, the lawyer made up a petition for succession of Pierre's estate. Knowing what was to come, Jules quietly resigned from his position before the summons arrived. He knew it would be explosive when they came to Madame Dejan demanding she prove that she was the sole heir of Pierre's estate.

When Jean Benjamin was served the papers, his eyes grew dark. In a fury he walked over to the store to see if Mama Dejan had also received a summons.

She sat behind the counter with the newly served petition, reading intently, glasses perched upon her nose. With the sound of Jean's footsteps, she paused.

"I see you were served too, Maman," Jean said.

"Who would have ever expected this," she said, tossing the papers aside. "Now I know why Jules left us so unexpectedly."

"Jules was behind it all."

"I know. He gave no solid reason for leaving without notice, which I found odd, for he is a very polite and fastidious man."

"Good manners can often be used as a distraction while less-than-honest matters are concluded. What I fear is that Jules knows everything about us."

"He can't win. We've done everything exactly as Mr. Theard instructed us."

"The brothers hope to find a chink in the armor, some small thing we've overlooked."

"So they will want an inventory, yes?"

"Oh, I'm sure. Everything you own will have to be documented and appraised. There will be no stone left unturned if Jules has anything to do with it."

Josephine looked away, then pulled a lace handkerchief from her sleeve and dabbed her eye. "It will all cost a great deal of money, and still, they don't have a chance of prevailing."

"Sadly, no. And I believe the court wouldn't find in their favor even if they did have a bona fide right because they're colored, and you, *Ma'mère*, are white. But what is of greatest concern to me is that the whole community will follow such a trial. My children will be in the center of it all. They don't stand a chance of living quietly and with dignity. They will never pass in this city again."

The Dejan brothers' filing suit was noted in the papers the next day because this act attacked the marriage of conscience, and, even more important, it questioned the validity of interracial marriages ratified during Reconstruction. Many families in the Quarter and Marigny would be watching closely to see if their own marriages held up in the new heavily Democrat courts.

Jean Benjamin was furious that the Dejan brothers dared to drag them all down in public for such a futile cause and its selfish ends. What goaded him most was that it would all play out under the eyes of former Confederates who were still fighting their lost war in this new and subtle way. They would be happy to see such a case so that the character of free coloreds might be revealed as immoral, manipulative, and greedy.

The lasting effect of such revelations would please the Confederates to no end, for they knew every light-skinned colored man or woman was trying to jump the fence. And simply revealing these family histories and the intermarriage of races would guarantee lasting consequences in such a small community as New Orleans. For if made public, even the lightest of them would never pass, nor would any of their blood relatives, proving there were indeed other ways to enslave human beings.

MADAME JOSEPHINE DEJAN

1887

J EAN BENJAMIN AND MADAME DEJAN CONSULTED MR. Theard, who was now on the bench. Judge Theard agreed to represent her personally in the trial, hoping to discourage that young upstart Labatt from systematically taking his clients' private life apart in public. Theard had overseen Madame Dejan's 1867 suit to place Pierre's debts in her hands, which included his half of the business. He understood the complex issues facing the older coloreds in New Orleans who had jumped through many legal hoops to protect their assets.

Already the Democrats were crafting legislation to prohibit interracial marriage again, returning the city to the way it was before the Civil War. Such a climate would be even more deadly because it would reveal Josephine and her daughter Florentine's marriage to colored men. The climate had become largely unsympathetic to such unions now, and should the judge to hear this Dejan suit sympathize with the Knights of the White Camellia, the couple's chances of prevailing would be debatable.

Mama Dejan and Jean Benjamin sat in Judge Theard's darkly paneled office. He had done a great deal of business over the years for many of his wealthy colored clients. In this enclave, privacy was vital to his clientele,

This petition document prepared by the Dejan Brothers' lawyer, Labatt, lays out the details of their suit against Mama Dejan for half of her assets.

85

which would rather remain as low profile as possible. Theard had become well known for his sympathies, yet somehow he remained powerful enough among Southern Democrats to be appointed to the bench. Before him lay the complaints of the Dejan brothers, written out in their lawyer's flowery script.

Theard leaned over his desk, shuffling the large pages written in various hands. "I must get down to your store. This chair has been in my office since before the war and my old bones require a softer seat." Theard handed Jean copies of the documents. "Now, we have two primary ways we may mount a good defense. First, we must prove the business was your property before Pierre died, which requires us to provide witnesses to testify to that fact. Then we will provide receipts, checks, accounts, and journals to support the testimony."

"That will not be difficult because we have all of that and much more," Jean replied. "Not only does this apply to Mama Dejan, but I fear my right to own property will be questioned, and we must be able to show such documents to prove ownership unquestionably."

"Excellent. The court can deny testimony, but the appellate courts are unquestionably required to recognize documentation, particularly if it is duly notarized." Jean studied the documents as Theard continued. "Another more interesting plan is to attack the Dejan brothers, proving they are not legal heirs. Our emphasis here is on legality, which is what the court wants before decisions can be made."

Jean listened, then added, "We all know their white father, Jules Dejan, was the controller at Citizens, and their mother, Marguerite Doubere, is unquestionably colored. This makes all four brothers, including Pierre, the illegitimate natural sons."

"Correct. Even though the father allowed them to take his last name, and he was often seen with them around town, he didn't marry their mother, nor did he adopt the boys. This is evidenced by his will, which left a healthy inheritance to their uncle to be distributed to the sons. All of this points to the fact that Jules, Antoine, and Victor are not legally recognized as being related to Pierre, and therefore they do not have any right to his estate."

"Pierre was afraid of just such a problem," Josephine said. "The whole community knows them."

"But outside Marigny they aren't well known, and Jules is white enough to pass. That's why his father taught him the accounting trade. Remember, Jules hopes to pass, and the brothers are equally light and thus avoid much attention. They don't want their parentage made public, that is sure, but fifty thousand is enough to betray themselves in public. It would indeed cast a long shadow over their father's memory too. But what they should fear most is his widow, Justine Guiraudi. She may have a great deal of resentment for her husband's mistress, Marguerite, and prefer the illegitimate sons did not testify either."

Jean added, "So the risks we take to keep the estate intact present a risk for them too."

"I am afraid this is the kind of trial in which no one really wins even if we do prevail. Once the cat is out of the bag, there will be no private life for anyone. The Dejan brothers are asking for far more than money from your family, Madame."

A pall hung over the Esnard home in the months leading up to the trial. They all felt violated as the Dejan brothers forced the details of their livelihood and marriages to become part of the public record.

"There's no way to know what the whites will do when they discover your mother's efforts to control her community property," Jean said over breakfast with Florentine on the eve of the court-ordered inventory.

"Would they call it a marriage of convenience, Jean? Would they call ours a marriage of convenience too?"

"At least we have the children, and I daresay quite a few of them, my dear. But your mother and Pierre were childless. An unnatural marriage, they would say, and therefore never blessed by God. It'll be hard to prove this union was anything more than a business arrangement."

"The white women will say my mother was punished for her ambitions. She worked in a man's world and didn't respect her husband as the master of the business."

"Theard is well aware of it. When the men come tomorrow with Jules to take the inventory, I will be there to help your mother. She must declare everything. She must be seen as scrupulously honest and forthright. I don't want them to suggest in any way that she's holding back."

The next day Jean Benjamin appeared at the store a full half hour before the inventory was to begin, knowing that Jules would also arrive early to make sure everything was counted. The store constituted a large two-story structure in which every square inch was packed with inventory. Much of it came from Pierre's early acquisitions after the war when whole households of furniture were auctioned. Those purchases were placed in storage until there was room for them in the showroom.

The inventory demanded by the brothers' attorney also included a full inventory of all Mama Dejan's assets. Not only would this disturb their life and business, but it was also a great threat to their personal privacy.

Everything in the house and store was to be inventoried, from Mama Dejan's pearl earrings to the appraisal of the house itself. The men arrived on time that morning and pried into everything, assigning value to each item and recording it page after page.

In one loft alone were over two hundred chairs, and toward the end the inventory officers finally set generalized value to such scenarios because it would take far too long to appraise every item. It was horribly disruptive, forcing Madame Dejan to her bed with headaches every afternoon. Somehow this legal challenge on top of her grief for Pierre made her grow older by the day. She seemed to suffer even more when the inventory dredged up the many loans she'd made as well as appraisal of all buildings she had bought as investments around the city. Jules was particularly attentive to ensure all were considered because real estate constituted the bulk of her wealth.

Florentine couldn't help defer her mother's duties because she had so many little ones. Jean Benjamin oversaw what he could at the store when not tending to his daily activities of collecting payments and rents, and scouting real estate investments. Mama Dejan had ceased reading the *Tribune* altogether after too many inaccurate quotes from Jules Dejan or his young lawyer found their way into print.

Paul Theard informed them that Labatt would call every adult in the family to the witness stand, so there were preparatory meetings in the lawyer's office as well. They discussed the rules of their testimony as it influenced a civil matter. Answer as briefly as possible. Do not volunteer any information. And, above all, maintain dignity at all times. "I would like you all to appear as calm and confident as possible. I will bring Jules to betray himself with anger by questioning the Dejan brothers' legitimacy."

DEJAN V. DEJAN

New Orleans, 1888

O N THE DAY THE CIVIL TRIAL BEGAN, MADAME DEJAN, Jean Benjamin Esnard, and his wife, Florentine, rode together in their buggy driven by one of the store employees. They stopped before the imposing new brick courthouse with its turrets and the grand clock tower that could be seen for miles above the rooftops of the city. The mild day was overcast, with the city unusually quiet because it was Lent. Easter was just a few weeks away, and the city waited in great anticipation to throw off its sackcloth and ashes.

Madame Dejan was met at the curb by Judge Theard, who made a grand gesture as she took his arm and mounted the steps to the new building. She stood straight and tall with a stylish bonnet bearing soft lavender silk flowers and Irish lace. Behind them followed Jean Benjamin in his finest suit, a cutaway that did nothing to hide his expanding waistline. One passerby clearly recognized Jean and tipped his hat toward the dour group making their way inside.

They settled in the front row as Judge Theard directed Madame Dejan through the gate to sit beside him at the defense table.

This page was excerpted from the original testimony in the *Dejan v. Dejan* succession case in which Judge Theard is questioning Jules Dejan II about his white father, Jules Dejan of Citizens Bank, and colored mother, Marguerite Doubere. It is a rare example of handwritten court reports. Such testimony of all members of this suit reveals their lives through actual testimony given.

89

This page from *Dejan v. Dejan* shows how documents were hand-copied when presented to the court as evidence. This is the will of white banker Jules Dejan I, leaving much of his property to his brother Octave, designated as a "universal legatee" of his estate. Because the sons were illegitimate, they could not inherit because the courts did not recognize them. The way colored families circumvented this problem was to appoint a white family member as universal legatee trusted to dole out assets as needed by the colored children.

The smell of newly sawn cypress still lingered in the fine paneling of the court now illuminated by south-facing windows. Josephine peeked around her attorney to see the three Dejan brothers sitting on the other side of the court with the young Labatt, and she could not help but notice how much they resembled her dearly departed Pierre. Her husband had been the lightest one of them all and, like Jules, often passed in unknown company as a white man.

It seemed as though the attorneys would go on forever with their long-winded opening statements. Judge Theard's oratory was flawless as he laid out the primary elements of the case. As their lawyer, he was involved with them every step of the way, from Josephine and Pierre's marriage of conscience in 1858 to the current succession suit. He went over every legal maneuver: the ratification of their marriage in 1867 followed by Josephine's suit against Pierre to take over his half of the estate. His words flowed like honey in a deep southern drawl from above the bushy white goatee. His posture was ramrod straight within a perfectly fitting frock coat that gave him the elegance of age compared to Labatt, who, though handsome enough and quite articulate, appeared less than a formidable opponent.

Then just when Theard's words had soothed them all into a half sleep, he sat down and Labatt called Jules Dejan to the stand.

How old are you, Mr. Dejan?
Fifty-six years old.
Where were you born?
New Orleans.
Did you know Pierre Dejan?
Yes.
When did he die?
He died . . . I think it was on the last day of October.

Where did he reside?
He resided at the corner of Dauphine and Barracks.
Was he any relation of yours?
Yes, sir, he was my brother.
Are your brothers, Victor and Arthur [Antoine], plaintiffs with you in this suit?
Yes, sir.
Did your brother Pierre leave any children?
No, sir.
Did he leave property and effects in New Orleans?
A furniture business.
Were you his bookkeeper up to the time of his death?
Yes, sir.
What was the character of the property at the corner of Dauphine and Bar-
racks Streets where your brother lived and died?
It was a regular furniture store, yes, sir.
Who carried the business? Who managed it?
My brother managed it.
Who made the purchases and sales for the business during this time?
My brother did.
How long had he been there, in the store?
Since the place was built until he died.
Do you know his wife, Mrs. Dejan?
Yes, sir.
Had she any separate industry to your knowledge?
Not to my knowledge, sir.
What part of the business did she attend to?
She managed the cash business at that time.
And he managed the customers and the sales?
Yes, sir.
What was the condition of your brother's health—was he an active and
industrious man?
Yes, sir, up to fifteen days before he died.

Jean knew that Labatt was hard at work leading Jules to lie about Pierre's activity in the store. Everyone knew that Madame was the manager. Pierre, so well known in Marigny neighborhoods, was strongly part of the welcoming effort that greeted every customer that entered the shop. This personal touch was quite important in the colored community because the white-owned stores tended to ignore people of color and then often acted as though it was a burden to take their money.

Then Judge Tissot invited Judge Theard to cross-examine the witness.

Theard stood and stepped out from behind his table, straightened his silk vest, and then pulled out his watch, taking note of the time. As he floated toward Jules, his brows knitted, he used his deepest voice to begin.

Mr. Dejan!

Jules jumped. The sudden booming voice startled him out of his gaze at someone in the back of the courtroom.

Do you dare to say that that store was carried on and conducted by your brother, Pierre Dejan?
Yes, sir.
Was Mr. Pierre Dejan's name on the door?
No, sir.

Theard glanced up at Tissot and smiled, and then he turned back to the witness.

What was the name on the door?
Madame Dejan.

Another wry smile.

What was the name used in the dealings with the public?
Just as I tell you—Mrs. Dejan.
In whose name were the bills made out?
Mrs. Dejan.
In whose name was the bank account?
There was for a very short time a bank account kept, but I know nothing about that I was not aware that there was a bank account kept until after the death of my brother.

Theard stepped back to lean against the defense table as he went on, one hand in his coat pocket.

Did you testify in the case of Madame Dejan versus her husband?
Yes, sir, in 1876, but when I testified in 1876, I wasn't aware of what I have discovered since the death of my brother.

Jules's otherwise confident manner was suddenly changed, and he did not speak with the same certainty. He attempted to prove he didn't know about the marriage of conscience, but his statement became convoluted.

I was informed by my brother and his wife that they were not married prior to 1869. They had worked together as strangers, partners, and the money, the amount she was claiming at that time in 1876 was the share acquired by her as partner of my brother. Now since the death of my brother, I have found out that I was not only in error, but the attorney in the case was just as I was. My brother was married in 1858, so my testimony in 1876 was contradictory of what I have found out since my brother's death.

This testimony, Theard knew, was vital, for unbeknownst at the time, he himself was the much younger attorney being referenced.

You say your brother was married in 1858?
Yes, sir.
And that is the object for which you introduced that document in evidence?
Yes, sir.
Was not Madame Dejan a white woman?
A subtle murmur rose from the courtroom audience.
Jules replied softly, *Yes, sir.*
Could they have married then in 1858?
Yes, sir, that marriage of 1858 has been legalized under the statute 258 of 1868.

Mr. Theard read from the testimony of Jules Dejan found in record 19815 of the docket of Civil District Court.

Labatt objected on the grounds that "Said judgments were fraudulent and simulated a cover for a voluntary separation."

He was overruled, and Theard continued with the legal suit that occurred just four months after Josephine and Pierre were legally married in 1876, the ratification of the earlier marriage of conscience. At that point Josephine stated that she was forced to buy up Pierre's bad debts. Such public testament of the debts would prove to the court that they were shifting ownership for business reasons. However, everyone was aware that such shifts were almost always about race, particularly when the spouse in question was not a criminal, gambler, or a drunk. Inability to pay his bills was the strategy used to prove Pierre was too irresponsible to manage the family's money.

Labatt again objected, stating that the separation of property was essentially bogus: "*This separation of property is absolutely null and void in its face . . . That it was rendered upon insufficient evidence and without hearing all the parties, as required by the Code. The judgment offered was not based on proof and was a fraud. The wife against the husband, like this, proof must be offered or it can produce no effect.*"

The statement was added to the court testimony, and then Theard continued.

Was that the testimony given by you in that suit in 1876?

Yes, sir.

Do you know whether there was a judgment rendered in that case?

Yes, sir.

In favor of Madame Dejan?

Yes, sir.

You say you kept the store's books before the separation of property and since the separation of property.

Yes, sir. For one year before.

You have always made those entries, charging against Mrs. Dejan and not Mr. Dejan?

Yes, sir, because the store was under Mrs. Dejan's name.

Satisfied, Theard thanked the court and returned to his seat. He whispered something to Josephine and then sat back in his chair, thumbs in his vest. Then Mr. Labatt announced he wished to reexamine his witness.

Mr. Dejan, was your brother in that store to your knowledge acting as a clerk or master?

As master all the time.

Did he receive any salary?

I never saw any.

Did he handle the money himself in the store?

Yes, sir, he was master of the place.

Following Jules's testimony, Theard called a number of other businessmen and former employees to the stand to validate that everything belonged to Josephine. More than once the witnesses told of giving money to Pierre and seeing him immediately hand it over to his wife. In each case, almost as if they had been coached, each quoted Pierre as saying to her, "Here is your money."

Then the case took another direction as Labatt sought to designate the Dejan brothers as legitimate heirs to their brother's estate. He again called Jules to the stand.

Mr. Dejan, when your brother died, had he any father and mother living?

No, sir.

Did they die before him?

Yes, sir.

Do you know whether he left any will or not that you ever heard of?

I have heard that he left no will.

You inquired?

I inquired, yes, sir.

Were you and your brothers friendly to the day of the death?
Friendly all the time.

Labatt retreated, and Theard stood again, this time with an air of antici-pation. Jules would not be taken off guard again, and his eyes never left the dark blue ones of Theard as the lawyer approached the stand.

Mr. Dejan, would you say that you and Victor and Arthur [Antoine] Dejan—the three plaintiffs—were the brothers of Pierre Dejan?
Yes, sir.
Were you the legitimate brothers of Pierre Dejan?

Theard clearly emphasized the word *legitimate*, for that was one of his primary points, and Jules had fallen right into the trap.

Yes, sir.
Do you understand the meaning of the word legitimate?
Yes, sir.
Who was your father?
Jules Dejan.
The gentleman who was the comptroller, I believe, of the Citizens Bank?
Yes, sir.
He was a white man, was he not?

This time the courtroom remained perfectly quiet.

Yes, sir.
Who was your mother?
Mrs. Doubere.
Was she not a colored woman?
She was stated so.

Theard stepped back to his table, feigned a peek at his paperwork, and then returned, his gaze pinned on Jules.

Now, Mr. Dejan, was she not a colored woman? There is no shame in being a colored man.

Jules grew sad, a look of futility replacing the former confidence. Now he would have to reveal everything.

No, sir, I am not ashamed of it.
Was she not a colored woman?
Yes, sir.
You are the eldest of the family?
Yes, sir.

How old are you?
Fifty-six.
So your youngest brother must have been born sometime about 1837.
Yes, sir.
Could your father, who was a white man, and your mother, who was a colored woman, contract a marriage at that time under the laws of Louisiana?
No, sir.

Then Theard went on to show how Jules's mother had died and his father remarried to a white woman ten years later. They then brought the father's will into evidence.

Did your father make any disposition in your favor, you and your brothers?
Yes, sir.

Theard frowned again, knowing the defendant was lying, so he repeated his question.

By his will?
Yes, sir.
By his will?

Theard's voice rose at the repeat of the question.

This excerpt from the trial transcript shows two things. At the top is a "note," which describes the marital status of Jules Dejan, the white father of the colored Dejan brothers. Further down is the start of Florentine Krach Esnard's testimony.

Not direct, but leaving to one of my uncles my share.
He left to one of his brothers, Octave. He left one-half of his estate to your uncle Octave, with the understanding that he would pay over to you the full sum?
Yes, sir.
Why did he do that?
Because at that time he could not will it directly.
He could not give you anything at that time?
No, sir.
Why, because you were his natural son?
Yes, sir.

Following this admission, Theard then spoke to the court on the matter of the Dejan brothers' illegitimacy and thus their natural relationship with Pierre was not legally valid. He then went on to point out that Madame

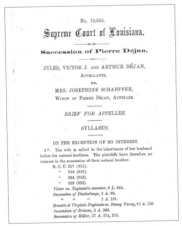

Later in her testimony Florentine Krach Esnard describes herself as the "Keeper of Funds" for Mama Dejan's store. This general mistrust of the banks was not uncommon with colored families during the latter nineteenth century.

No. 10,055.

Supreme Court of Louisiana.

Succession of Pierre Déjan.

JULES, VICTOR J. AND ARTHUR DÉJAN,
APPELLANTS,
vs.
MRS. JOSEPHINE SCHAEFFER,
WIDOW OF PIERRE DÉJAN, APPELLEE.

BRIEF FOR APPELLEE.

SYLLABUS.

ON THE EXCEPTION OF NO INTEREST.
1°. The wife is called to the inheritance of her husband
before his natural brothers. The plaintiffs have therefore no
interest in the succession of their natural brother.
R. C. C. 917 (911).
"   919 (913).
"   924 (918).
"   929 (923).
Victor vs. Tagiasco's executor, 6 L. 644.
Succession of Duclozlange, 2 A. 98.
"   "   1 A. 181.
Monette & Virginia Duplessis vs. Betsey Young, 11 A. 120
Succession of Brisco, 2 A. 268.
Succession of Miller, 27 A. 574, 375.

Following the verdict, the attorney for the Dejan brothers appealed many aspects of the trial in a series of briefs that would eventually lead to final decision, in favor of Mama Dejan by the Louisiana Supreme Court.

Dejan was legally married to Pierre, twice in fact, and that she is *"purely, simply and unconditionally the successor of her said husband and to be sent and put in possession thereof. Wherefore she prays that this exception be maintained and the suit of plaintiffs dismissed."*

No dismissal was made, and the trial continued with the submission into evidence a number of documents proving that Madame Dejan indeed owned the store, the real estate, and the notes loaned out for mortgages. Despite Labatt's efforts to examine Victor and Antoine Dejan about their recollections of the couple's business relationship, they could not produce a single document to prove their case. In the process even their father's will was introduced by Theard showing he did not will anything directly to his sons, which proved that at least in the father's estimation he had no marriage and they were indeed illegitimate.

As the trial finally wound down, the papers were already calling the verdict, but there had been a great deal of editorial on the notion of shifting of assets from colored members of the family to that of the whites and how this could interfere with succession. An undercurrent in many of the reports suggested it was an unusual case to find white women married into colored families, and letters to the editor by Confederates on that matter were not complimentary.

During the long period of the trial, Mama Dejan would provide a great deal more documentation of all their real estate holdings and other assets down to the horse and wagon used in the store deliveries. Such an extensive inventory would lay open every aspect of the Esnard-Dejan family from where they kept their cash to the legal survey of every building or lot they owned. However, they drew the line when it came to loans made by Jean Benjamin on Mama Dejan's behalf to colored residents with little chance of receiving a traditional loan from white-controlled banks.

When Judge Tissot finally found the case in favor of Madame Dejan, they all breathed a sigh of relief that the circus would be over and they could return to life as it was before Pierre's death. But sadly the entire family became far too well known, and what was revealed in the course of such a legal battle would forever remain in the public record. No Esnard or Dejan would ever be able to jump the fence.

Before long, they were again notified that the upstart Labatt had appealed the verdict and that Theard would have to argue the case once again.

In one meeting with Jean Benjamin and Madame Dejan, Judge Theard said, "I doubt there will be any overturn of this case because there is simply not enough evidence. Labatt wants to remain in the public eye, for already he has moved to a nicer part of town. Should he fail in his appeal, he will go to the Supreme Court of Louisiana, and then who knows? Perhaps to Washington. But Labatt will likely be satisfied to keep it all in this state because that is where he will benefit most."

Theard was correct, for the case dragged on another year in the appeals process, which kept him busy responding to Labatt's specious arguments and flood of paperwork. Though the furniture store became more famous than ever, Madame Dejan had grown self-conscious and was never again comfortable outside her home. She began to feel as though the city saw her as the symbol of the inherent immorality of interracial marriage. As a proud French-born businesswoman, this caused her no shame, but she could not ignore the tone of the city now changed by immigrants and Democrats. Many felt that white women should not take any interest in colored men. Even to glance at one was a breach of moral etiquette. Only prostitutes and those of low moral standing who could not find a white husband would stoop to marrying a colored man. Mama Dejan did not just worry for herself but for Florentine's reputation as well. Her daughter was destined to the same fate.

But from the day the trial of *Dejan v. Dejan* opened, all of New Orleans came to know the names, and life afterward was never quite the same. And though Madame Dejan was white and now a widow, there was the unspoken belief that her marriage would make her the socially colored equal of her husband. This placed doubt on exactly where she and Florentine belonged in restaurants, streetcars, and other public places. Should she be accused of violations, she would be arrested and sentenced to thirty days in city jail.

PART VII
JIM CROW

ADRIEN BENJAMIN ESNARD

1890

FTER THE TRIAL, JEAN BENJAMIN BEGAN LOOKING for real estate opportunities outside the city. He and Mama Dejan both agreed it would be best for them all if they could get away from the constant scrutiny.

On one fall day after the deathly heat of summer had ebbed, Jean set out in a buggy with his eleven-year-old son, Adrien. Smaller than his older brothers, this dark studious child needed some personal attention. They would cross the river and explore the now-destitute plantations that once lined the River Road with prosperity.

"I want to see this farm, Adrien, that's up for auction. It was owned by the Cazillards before the war, and now there's a chance for us to buy it."

"What did they grow there, Père?"

"Sugarcane, mostly. But I don't think the fields have been replanted in years. The house is just behind the levee, and it would make a good place for your mama to spend the summer. She doesn't manage the city so well now and the girls need relief too."

The Cazillard Plantation house at Algiers on the River Road became the summer getaway for the Esnards after the trial. It would be one of the last properties sold by the family, well after their move to Los Angeles.

Their horse clopped down the famous old road that had seen armies march through the War of 1812. "This is where they fought the battle of New Orleans,"

100

Jean narrated. "And here is the point where Farragut's fleet met the Confederate ships. There were Yankees camped all over this side of the river for years. Only their captains lived in the city. When your grand-père and I joined the Union army, we marched along this road and camped up in those trees yonder. They gave me the drum, and I beat the cadence of their footsteps. It was a glorious time during that war, but we didn't see much fighting around these parts."

Adrien listened with rapt attention, his dark eyes glittering with an innate intelligence and love of history. Long tresses of Spanish moss swayed from the passing of their buggy beneath great live oaks that lined both sides of the road. Their shadows cast out far across the grassy ground that flanked the crushed shell surface. Far beyond, sugarcane was a bright green ribbon on the horizon. Occasional glints in the sun marked the places where workers swung their cane knives.

Finally they reached the destination, a single old house standing a hundred yards beyond the road. It stood on thick brick piers that fronted a more substantial brick footing that bound the entire ground floor. "The river once flooded here," Jean said. "Every year these old places stood in the water and the boats came to get the people, takin' them from one place to the other. Now we got levees, so the high water rarely comes this far anymore."

Adrien studied the long porch that ran across the front of the place, but it was not the classical imposing Greek revival columns of the grand houses. These were simple farmhouse posts, turned on the ends and made of cypress to last. The roof sloped toward him from its peak, shingles buckled here and there around two dormers, each bearing a single shuttered window. It looked to the boy like a sleeping French bulldog, its eyes nearly shut and the lips revealing a few irregular teeth as it dozed on the riverbank.

Jean pointed northward toward a string of listing fence posts. "That fence there was the north line of the British Army. They didn't get any farther than that in the Battle of New Orleans. When they fell, Andy Jackson's general, David Morgan, kept this line right here at Cazillard and stayed in this very house, his men billeted all over these fields."

"What's that little brick house way out there, Père?"

"That there's the sugarhouse and beside it is the mill where they crushed the cane. That's all that's left. Folks stole everything they could after the war just to get by, and what was left might have been carried off by high water."

They climbed out of the carriage, and Jean tied their horse to a ring embedded in one of the oaks in front of the house. The tree's thick, scaly bark had completely consumed the heavy chain, leaving only the last link visible, from which the ring dangled. Father and son walked through the grass to the empty house that seemed more derelict the closer they got. The once-white paint peeled and in some places was gone altogether to reveal the cypress lapboards below. Upon closer inspection, they could see the front porch listing slightly south. They walked around to the end of the porch and climbed rickety steps that groaned under Jean's considerable weight. The front door squealed from its hinges as they pushed it open.

Inside the house was cool and dark, with a rich smell of wood smoke, bacon grease, dust, and rodents nesting in the attic. The great front room was dominated by a large fireplace, the brick wall above blackened with a century of soot. Clearly no one had lived there for some time, evidenced by the dry leaves that had collected in the corners and the windowsills layered with silt.

Adrien explored each room on the ground floor and climbed a ladder into the attic, where he could hear scurrying sounds, and dust motes danced upon shafts of light coming in through the broken shingles. Then together they went downstairs to inspect the brick basement, dark as a tomb and smelling of earth and mold.

Their explorations completed, father and son sat on the porch steps, eating cheese and bread they had brought and looking out at the muddy river flowing by. "What do you think, Adrien Benjamin? Shall we buy this ol' house?"

"Ma'mère will say it's dirty, but I like it very much. Do you think anyone else will make a bid on the place?

"Perhaps not. You see, New Orleans is a city built on favors and money. Sometimes you can gain something of value by returning a favor. Other times a bit of money can cut through to open the way more cleanly. There is a good man at the bank, a fine chess player I might add. He repossessed this property and told me over a game the other day. I believe I may be able to convince him to skip the auction and sell this place to me directly."

"Père, will we plant cane again? I'd like to see how it is done. That huge old pot in the sugarhouse must need a big fire."

"Takes a lot of wood, and that means you need to cut and haul it. That costs a lot of money now. Before the war, things was different out here. They had slaves. It was a bad time for them."

"It feels good out here, don't it, Père? Feels like we've been livin' here a thousand years."

"I believe you're right, boy. Maybe we can put this old house together again and live here a thousand more."

CAZILLARD PLANTATION

RIVER ROAD, ALGIERS, LOUISIANA

1891

SUMMER DESCENDED ON THE GULF COAST AS MAMA Dejan closed the store and the Esnards packed up their things, preparing to cross the river to Algiers. In a great caravan of wagons they rumbled out of the city. Florentine was newly pregnant with her eighth and last child. She rode in the two-seat family buggy with her daughters. Her two youngest were Marie Florentine, simply known as Flo, and Marie Josephine, named for her grandmother. Jo, as she was called, was the darkest girl, her almond-shaped eyes and rich skin color distinctly exotic. Jean often remarked how much she resembled his late mother, Marie Louise Smith. The oldest girl, Adrienne, was the spitting image of her mother and resembled her in personality as well. She sat in the last seat beside Mama Dejan, who had aged considerably over the past year.

Rene, Adrien, Paul Filbert, and Raoul all rode in the supply wagon that followed the women's buggy. Each of them was sheltered from the sun by woven palm leaf hats favored by cane workers.

Jean Benjamin had gone ahead with furnishings sent from the store to supervise the workers who had been hired to clean and repair the house and drive out all forms of vermin that thrived along the river. Their cook was there to shop and supply the pantry as well as grapple with the old iron cook stove that was a great improvement over the hearth fireplace. Jean's aim was to make the home as comfortable as possible because both his wife and her mother had suffered during the many months of trial and appeal. They had become more and more housebound, fearing the disapproving looks of those not familiar with the more liberal racial milieu of the Marigny community.

When the wagons rolled off the River Road into the front yard, they found the house freshly whitewashed and the listing porch shimmed back to level. The treads on the staircase were new again, and inside the women found the old woodwork gleaming with fresh oil. Both smiled for the first time in months, proving this haven on the river was more than just a refuge from summer fever season in the city. It would become their sanctuary, isolated and free of prying eyes and flapping tongues. Here they could rest and recover.

On the river, Adrien followed Raoul and Paul Filbert everywhere they went. The three explored the wooded banks both up- and downstream, wandered the cane fields, and occasionally walked into Algiers. They grew nut brown in the sun, but Paul Filbert, with his mother's pale complexion, always wore a wide-brimmed hat because his face was pink with heat. They explored buildings left abandoned after the war, some of them mere blackened relics. On lands formerly the property of much larger plantations, they would find slave quarters with mud hearths and the grisly artifacts of slavery.

Jean Benjamin gave the boys a small German shotgun. He'd join them in the early morning, sitting in their carefully constructed duck blind, which the boys had fitted with an old but comfortable chair for their portly father. Together they drank lukewarm French chicory coffee, waiting for the birds to fly, sometimes in silence but more often while discussing how they might live in the future with the degenerating political conditions for the colored class. Supper was fish or birds, and the Esnards enjoyed a life only dreamed of by Simeon or Etienne. They lived in the old master's house there on the river during those languid summer days.

The girls remained snow white beneath their wide hats or, sequestered in the shade, their bodies swathed in white linen. Much of the time they sat thoroughly netted against the mosquitoes. There wasn't so much for them to do out there on the river, and more than once they longed to be back in the city with music and shops and friendships. But during the summer the social season slowed to a halt as everyone abandoned everyday life to remain cool and well. When friends and family came out to their river house, particularly Jean Benjamin's many brothers and sisters, the girls picnicked on the riverbank and waded into the backwater in the heat of the day, their gauze water dresses floating on the slow-moving current.

It was their second or third summer on the river that changed everything for Adrien. His voice had begun to crackle mid-sentence. A dark shadow of whiskers appeared on his smooth face. So busy was he with hunting and fishing that he neglected to keep his hair cut and suitably oiled. It fluffed up into golden wool.

That was when Florentine realized they had a problem as she was pack-ing the girls' things to return to the city. This middle boy, the bright and stu-dious one, had changed, and she had been too busy that summer to realize it. He was growing differently than the other boys, and she noticed the resem-blance to one brother of Jean Benjamin in particular. The African blood of Louise that flowed in his veins grew more obvious after a long summer in the sun. It was certain he was not a black man, but Adrien was unmistakably not white either. Age had widened his nose, and his lips had filled out sensually like those hidden beneath Jean Benjamin's mustache. No one in Louisiana would mistake Adrien for a white child, and he would not pass even in the most liberal circles.

Late that evening Florentine sat out on the porch with Jean watching the children playing atop the levee, their lithe bodies silhouetted in the setting sun.

"Have you looked closely at Adrien, Jean? He's changing."

"Why of course. He is becoming a man."

"It is not that," she said, then lowered her voice to a whisper. "He's so much darker than the others. He'll never pass."

Jean looked out at the river, then combed his oiled hair back with large, strong fingers. "You are so wise, Florentine. I didn't see it at all, but now that you mention it, I guess I just didn't want to admit it to myself. I should have expected at least one of them to resemble my family."

"It's not so much Adrien's future that concerns me, Jean. It's the girls.'"

"What is so wrong with that, *mon chérie?*" Jean said in jest, knowing exactly what she intimated. "After all, you married me knowing all my broth-ers were dark."

"That was another time, Jean. You know that. As if the trial was not bad enough, now they passed that horrible law. My girls can't marry at all."

Jean's face fell. "Oh, yes, the law."

"They can't marry a white man or they violate the law. And if they marry a colored man, they'll become just like me and my mother. We can't even go out to eat anymore because you're barred from whites-only establishments. As your wife, so am I."

"I don't think Adrien's appearance would make any difference. Every-body knows who we are now after all the newspaper coverage of the trial. The Esnard and Dejan families and our private business became common knowledge."

"That's where you're wrong, Jean. I'm afraid Adrien would be demoral-ized when he couldn't find work."

"He can always find employment in the store, my love."

"There's another problem too. Should the girls marry a white man here or elsewhere, they could have a colored child like Adrien. I can't imagine what difficulty that would cause."

A tear ran down Florentine's face. "What have we done, Jean, creating these children?"

"They are a gift of God, my dear." Jean pulled a white handkerchief from his back pocket and dabbed her cheeks gently with the corner. "Now dry your tears. We should rejoice to have them so healthy and strong."

Florentine wiped her eyes, frowning that tears had stained her shawl between two embroidered red roses. "It's just that . . . that my girls are destined to become old maids, Jean. I'll never be able to give them a wedding."

Jean leaned over to hug his wife as she wept. He lifted her chin up to look into those pale gray eyes. "It is our love, my dear, that created all of those beautiful lives out there. They will learn to make their own way in the world just like we did."

A week after their return to the city, Florentine walked to St. Augustine Church to visit Father Subileau. The housekeeper ushered her into the rectory parlor and motioned for her to take a seat on the davenport where she would be more comfortable than the hardwood chairs.

Moments later, Father Subileau came into the room bearing his characteristic smile that revealed small yellowed teeth. His dark eyes twinkled beneath brown hair carefully combed over his balding head. Thin and slightly hunched, his cassock didn't fit quite right, but his intensity proved a great life force dwelled within the small middle-aged parish priest.

"Madame Esnard," he said holding out his bony hand. "How good it is to see you again. Your contribution of the new lectern is much appreciated."

"That was my mother's donation, Père. She's a generous woman and quite devoted to St. Augustine."

"And we to her, Madame. So what brings you here this fine day? I sense you are struggling with a dilemma."

"Père, my husband doesn't know I'm here so please keep the visit to yourself. It's Adrien."

Father Subileau thought for a moment, trying to mentally place the boy, then realized instantly why Madame Esnard was there.

"He must be the bright one who was confirmed last year."

"That's the one. He's becoming a man as you well know."

"Yes, I saw him at Mass on Sunday. Considerably darker after his summer on the river."

Florentine looked down, embarrassed that the priest had already noticed, which instantly validated her worst fears. "You noticed, so the whole city will notice too. I don't want him to have trouble, Père. He's so intelligent and sensitive. There's no future for him in Louisiana except pain." Tears began to well up in her eyes, but she took a deep breath and held them back.

"Not an uncommon problem, Madame. You aren't the only family in our parish with such difficulties. Many parents have come to see me because of the new marriage law and what it means for their own children. It's a horrible thing. All we can do is try to educate our youngsters so they can find quality work. These days the laboring class is so full of new immigrants and newly freed fieldworkers."

"I don't want Adrien to grow up here."

"Many young men are leaving for Europe so they may study a profession without attending the poor colored schools. With God's blessing we hope they'll return one day to find a good life here. Adrien may follow that path too. You're wealthy enough to easily pay his tuition at the *petite seminarie*, something more difficult for our poorer families."

"I understand all of that, but the problem is me. It is so difficult to send a child so far away."

Florentine pulled a small handkerchief from her sleeve and dabbed her eyes.

"It's less painful to consider it only a brief separation, Madame. He'll come back when his schooling is over."

"But Adrien idolizes his older brothers. He won't want to leave them."

"That's because he knows nothing else. Perhaps if you bring him here, I may be able to encourage him to go."

"Do you think that's possible?"

"Adrien is a studious boy and one of the best scholars at the Jesuit school. That's in our favor. A boy with such a good mind will respond to my descriptions of the great cathedrals and the cities of Europe he's only read about in books. And then there are symphonies and universities and, of course, the King of Belgium too."

"I suppose he would be interested in all that. He's forever asking me and my mother questions about our childhood in Alsace."

"Your timing may be perfect, Madame, because I'm called back to our motherhouse in Brussels. The ship sails next month. If God is willing and places the desire in this boy's heart, I'll take him with me so we travel together.

I'll make it seem like a great adventure so that departing won't be so painful."

Florentine twisted her gold wedding band on her finger, then dabbed her eyes again and tucked the kerchief back into her sleeve. "I would like to see him become a doctor," she added. "Jean says he has an aptitude for it. The boy has the heart of a healer. As you know, a doctor will always have work no matter what color he is."

❦

It was a foggy morning when the store buckboard rolled up the toe of the levee where the stevedores were loading the hold of a large ship at anchor on the river. Behind the buckboard Jean and Florentine followed in the buggy with Adrien dressed in a tailored wool suit. His hair was well oiled and combed back from his forehead, making the dark brows and somber eyes more intense. They stepped out as the hired man removed a large steamer trunk from his buckboard and turned to Florentine for instruction.

"Please take that trunk down to the loading dock," Florentine said, noticing the black cassock of the approaching priest flap in the gentle morning breeze. She took a deep breath to hold back her tears because letting one of her babies go was not in her nature. Florentine reveled in being a mother and, though a taskmaster, inside she was an instinctive nurturer.

"Here is your escort, Adrien," Jean announced, the ever-present cigar clenched in his teeth as he spoke.

Florentine reached for her husband's arm, her normally rigid posture visibly melting as she realized that she wouldn't see her son for many years to come. Adrien sensed this and stepped over to her, taking her hand in his and softly kissing it. "Don't be sad, Maman. I won't be gone for long, right, Father?

Jean smiled but said nothing to validate Adrien's assumption. They all knew it was a long way to Belgium, making visits to the boarding school not only expensive but time consuming.

Then the ordinarily stalwart Florentine began to falter, her face etched with sadness almost as though her son had died. Jean's arm slipped around her corseted waist, and she threw herself into his arms, bursting into tears. "It's just not fair!" she cried, then hid her face in Jean's broad chest.

Jean's hand gently stroked her hair, then turned her face to his. "Remember the boy, Florentine," and she grew silent, reaching into her heart for strength. "It's a great adventure, so don't spoil it for him." Jean knew that Adrien would react to his mother's agony, and he didn't want a last-minute change of plans if the boy refused to board the ship. He stroked the buttons on the back of Florentine's dress until she gathered herself, wiped her face, and managed to hide her regret.

Father Subileau had kept Adrien's attention on the ship as his mother recovered enough to say good-bye and watch them board. She stood stone-faced at the top of the levee, arm in arm with her husband. It was far more difficult than she'd anticipated, and once the ship sailed, they went home, where Florentine shed an ocean of tears.

FLORENTINE KRACH-ESNARD

1894

MAMA DEJAN LIVED ALL ALONE IN THE NEW TOWN-
house next to the store. It seemed so large and empty without him. She
found no comfort in the soaring ceilings or the fine plasterwork, and
each piece of the furniture he chose for their house reminded her of Pierre
and his always-smiling face and gentle ways.

Florentine three years prior had given birth to a boy, whom she named
Marcel. Now she and Jean Benjamin had seven children living in their small
apartments behind the store. Something had to change, so Jean began looking for a larger house to rent.

The Esnards rarely ventured into the newer parts of New Orleans, which
were mostly white and populated by European immigrants and old Confederate families. Jean instructed his sons on the
latest law to impact their perpetually nar-
rowing freedoms. It stated in no uncertain
terms that a colored man having relations
with a white woman, whether or not by her
own free will, constituted a charge of rape.
This placed Jean in a precarious position
with a white wife. The boys were warned not
to look at any woman with a pale complexion because that too was now considered an
offense.

Family notoriety in an increasingly hostile racial climate had resulted in fewer customers from white neighborhoods across

A later portrait of Florentine
Krach-Esnard.

town. French furniture had gone out of style with the flood of Americans into the city. A number of new factories were churning out mass-produced American-style furnishings at a startling rate.

Finally Mama Dejan announced that she would move her things to the small bedroom over the kitchen to allow the rest of her family to move into the townhouse. She was lonely without Pierre, and her bedroom was too large for just one person. She longed to hear the sound of children in her house, which had become as silent as a tomb. She also needed someone there if she should take a fall or needed personal assistance. Before the trial she went to work at the store every day, but now Mama Dejan spent more time at home reading or taking long afternoon naps. Florentine suspected she suffered from melancholia brought on by the stress of the trial, increasing racial segregation, and the decline of their Old World community.

Florentine herself was somewhat of a taskmaster, though she was highly affectionate with her children. She found it uncomfortable to live under her mother's thumb. But after the trial, Mama Dejan's fiery way became far easier to live with, so the Esnards and their seven children moved into 1309 Dauphine Street, giving Florentine and Jean Benjamin the spacious master suite.

Due to decline in the business, Jean had become involved in the Louisiana Lottery Agency and was busy with its many endeavors, which placed him back in the eye of the political hurricane. At the same time, he remained in charge of managing investments for Mama Dejan. More and more he too felt the constraints of race in the Quarter growing even more claustrophobic than it was before the war. He was fully aware of the lynching and activities of the White League that went unprosecuted throughout Louisiana. Such threats of violence were nearly as deadly as slavery, he believed, and Jean knew he and his family were in jeopardy.

Jean Benjamin saw many of his own brothers leave town for a better life in northern states, where factories were in need of labor. They left because there was no hope of education or of racial freedom in Louisiana under the stranglehold of Jim Crow legislation. Jean's best hope for his own sons was for them to attend university and learn a profession that allowed them self-employment. Finding jobs as colored men put them in direct competition with a flood of white immigrants.

Perhaps more cause for worry was the futures of Adrienne, Flo, and Jo, Florentine's three daughters who had reached the age of majority. In Florentine's mind, the only way to keep them safe was to discourage them from marrying at all.

But what really concerned her most, what haunted her dreams, was the fact that any one of her own children could give birth to a dark child. If another child managed to pass in New Orleans or anywhere else for that matter, the darker sibling could cause a marital rift. If they remained in the city where the Esnards lived, such a child would also have to bear the family history of the Dejan trial. Florentine had seen it all over the Quarter with other families of mixed race who, through the fickle whims of recessive genes, wrecked havoc upon those light enough to jump the fence to white freedoms.

For both Jo and Flo, their religious convictions would cause them the greatest worry. The only option for the girls should they not marry was to enter the convent, but none of them had the desire to become religious. Florentine worried that suggesting a daughter not marry or subtly discouraging it would be a sin to be sure, but that sin paled in comparison to what could happen if one of them fell in love. So naturally, Florentine kept Adrienne, Flo, and Jo under her thumb so that there was no chance of meeting eligible men.

When Paul Filbert came home one day with Christine Brechtel on his arm, Florentine was not pleased. This white girl from a German immigrant family was a fine choice to be sure, but Paul Filbert was legally colored, though he easily passed. Florentine knew it was illegal for them to marry. At the time, Paul was apprenticed to a jeweler on Royal Street, where he was being trained as an engraver.

Then one evening Paul paid a visit to his parents, and they were in the parlor after dinner sipping sherry when he said, "We want to leave the city, Christine and I."

"You mean leave New Orleans? And go where?" Florentine set her glass gently on the table and turned all of her attention to the young man.

"It's the only way. We need a fresh start in a new city where we aren't known. I am as white as Flo, and I'd have no problems passing in Baton Rouge. We can start there fresh with no one knowing our family history. I would like to open my own store."

"But it is still illegal for you to marry her now," Jean Benjamin said. "You are crossing a dangerous line."

"I know that, Papa. But you know that the case of Monsieur Plessy forces me to ride in a separate streetcar from my wife. And they have separated the schools, and those for colored children are abysmal. I want my children to attend the white schools and grow up with those children. I want them to make friends with those who can help them in work and in society."

"Baton Rouge is still Louisiana, *mon fils*." Jean warned. "What if you have a child like Adrien? How will you explain it to the white families?"

"With each generation there is less and less chance of it."

"But, son, the risk is still there. If they discover that you have lied, it will be the end of you."

"It is already the end for my sisters. What if I have a daughter—will she deny marriage for this same fear? They don't know us in Baton Rouge. I'm willing to take the risk because the alternative is unacceptable. Please, Ma'mère and Papa, give us your blessing."

Florentine looked away, her lips pursed. Jean finished his sherry in one gulp and went to the decanter and refilled it to the brim. They sat in silence, knowing they could not stop Paul Filbert, who had fallen head over heels for the Brechtel girl.

"Then we shall go anyway," Paul said, standing to leave.

"Paul, how can your mother bless something that could result in your death? It's a real threat that's growing every day. They don't take kindly to lies."

"I have no choice. We won't live here like prisoners waiting for every new law to take more and more of what we have. They already tried and we prevailed, but now we live with those consequences. I love you both, but I must try to find a better life for my children." Paul left his parents alone.

Jean turned to Florentine. "The boy is right. I didn't want to tell you that they would not let me in the absinthe house yesterday. They're preparing a public accommodation statute that will forbid me from entering public houses. They want to make it illegal for coloreds and whites to drink together."

Florentine was shocked. "So how will you do business? Where will you go to meet your friends for chess?"

"For the white folks it must be elsewhere, perhaps in their homes. It's bad enough I must enter some restaurants through the kitchen, but now they say I can't be served a drink either. It's a five hundred dollar fine or two years in jail if I don't comply. How many business deals have I made over a good bottle of Bordeaux?"

The two aging parents sat alone in the parlor, suddenly feeling as defeated as Mama Dejan. Not only had race driven them to send Adrien away, but now Paul Filbert would also be leaving for the same reason. "What happened to all the good work we did after the war? How could they take our constitution apart like that?"

"They are afraid, Jean. They're small men who fear us. That's how people react when they are so uncertain of themselves that they must destroy anyone who might prove strong enough to contradict them."

"All but two of my brothers have gone north. My sisters have married into St. Cyr, Belot, Chesse, and Mirabin's families. Soon there will be none of us left under the Esnard name."

"Perhaps that is not such a bad thing. Those families of color are cursed by our name, which is well known and not so common that it could be overlooked. I've heard that many younger people are taking new surnames so they can separate themselves and their families from their own colored roots so they can pass too."

"Whether it works or not remains to be seen."

"Perhaps Paul Filbert is right, Jean. Maybe it's time for us to find a new city where no one knows our history. Mama is growing old and won't live forever. After she is gone, what then for us?"

PART VIII

BELGIUM

---✤---

ADRIEN BENJAMIN ESNARD

Brussels, 1894

NOW WAS FALLING WHEN THE BOAT DOCKED IN ANT-
werp. They had taken a steamer across the Atlantic, then a smaller riv-
erboat to the great city where Father Subileau was born. As he stepped
out onto the quay, the old bearded priest's eyes twinkled with joy at seeing his
homeland again. "Now we take a carriage to le petite seminarie at St. Nicho-
las," he said to Adrien, who stood beside him tightly wrapped in a wool sailor's
coat and neck scarf. "But first we shall buy you some proper winter clothing."

Their cab wove its way through the narrow streets to various stores
where Father Subileau replaced Adrien's light wardrobe for the heavy coats,
pants, underwear, and shoes better suited to the cold Belgian winter. When
they pulled up in front of the hulking stone school with its many wings and
towers, Adrien was already missing the warm comfort of New Orleans.
Europe was just as his mother and the priest had described, but they did not
tell him how cold it would be nor how early darkness fell in the winter.

Once in school, Adrien did not have much time to miss his family
because every day he was busy learning the difficult local language, Flemish
Dutch. Fortunately most of the Belgians in that bilingual country officially
spoke French just as Adrien had from birth. It was at night that he longed
to go home, as he lay under a thick feather comforter far from the coal stove
that heated the large room poorly. It was then, in the silent darkness, that he
realized he was alone in this strange new world.

He often awoke late at night after vivid dreams of the cane fields and the
great green river that flowed beyond the levees. Somehow it was all so soft
and languid, the voices smooth in their cadence, smells rich and fertile. They
seemed so sensual compared to the biting Dutch and German tongues and

the colorless winter, the women so drab in their blues and grays compared to the bright fabrics preferred back home.

When he felt most despondent, the only daytime cure was to walk to one of the many fine cathedrals in Antwerp, where brightly colored stained-glass windows reminded him of happy days at St. Augustine's. Adrien sat before a statue of the Blessed Mother dreaming of Florentine's tender touch. He often spoke to the Virgin in most intimate terms, finding comfort in her painted smile, soft blue eyes, and outstretched arms. He yearned to climb into them and reclaim the love and affection he had left behind to soften the regimented days at school.

Though this new life in Europe was not as his mother described, Adrien's young brain was awakening. He was surrounded by a new whirling universe of people and letters, of ancient cities and science. As the winter holiday approached, he looked forward to visiting his aunt Pauline, now married to Emil Biche, and the remnants of the Schaeffer family. He prayed to the Virgin that they would be able to fill at least part of the enormous hole in his heart.

Adrien did not go home at the end of the year. With each new term, his memories of New Orleans grew more vaporous, the river house fading from his mind. He had become close to Pauline's little sons, François and Andre, who were so like Adrien's brothers that they gave him much comfort. He told them stories about his exotic home in America, which seemed to increase his longing. Adrien became closer to some of the boys in his classes, sometimes joining them for holidays at their country houses. They'd often discuss attending the Belgian University of Louvain, one of the finest institutions of higher learning in Europe.

By the time Adrien was ready for university, New Orleans was but a distant memory. He had become fluent in Dutch, his French growing far more metropolitan. Like the other students, Adrien began taking weekend trips to Louvain to hear the speeches. There was unrest brewing for King Leopold II's activities in the Congo Free State. They had all read about it in the newspapers, and it came up for discussion many times in Adrien's classes.

They would all learn that rubber was essential to the industrial revolution and the fledgling automobile industry. Though rubber tree plantations had been started in colonial farms all over the tropical world, they had not matured sufficiently to produce a crop. The only reliable source in the interim was a certain vine that grew in the African equatorial jungle. To exploit such profits, King Leopold II managed to obtain the entire region of the Congo as his personal property. This constituted roughly twenty percent of the African land mass. Congo Free State was not a colony, as Adrien had thought at first, for it was not possessed by Belgium itself. As private owner, making himself king of Congo as well as Belgium, Leopold could act with impunity. He would stop at nothing to quickly harvest its botanical liquid gold.

Rumors said the king raided the prisons for men to do the job. Cruel and criminal in nature, these men would stop at nothing to increase their own self worth. Leopold sent them upriver from Leopoldville to facilitate rubber-gathering. These unscrupulous men encountered the native tribes and used any means necessary to obtain the precious resource.

Once established as a perennial student at Louvain, ostensibly study-ing medicine, Adrien could not help but become caught up in the political climate of that difficult time in Belgium. He would recall much of what his father, Jean Benjamin, had told him about those days before the American Civil War and his crucial role in Reconstruction politics.

After classes, students would go to the coffeehouses to discuss the bal-ance of power between the monarchy and the proponents of democracy. Adrien preferred a small coffeehouse on a corner behind the cathedral where the customers often discussed theology as well.

"Wasn't it just that way in your homeland, Hadriann?" a Norwegian stu-dent, Lars, asked, his accent thick and mel odious as he struggled with his French.

Adrien's opinion was always valued for his uniquely American point of view. "I'm not proud of how they treated slaves before the war, but it's not easy to find workers for the cane fields in the summer. I know the planters used violence to make them work. It was the only way to keep those farms in cultivation."

"Are you saying it must be justifiable if free workers can't be used?"

"Never. Such suffering is never justifiable. What the king is doing in Congo is the very same thing, perhaps worse. In Louisiana a slave had some value, for he could be sold, therefore it was not wise to damage him too badly. But in Congo the people have no value at all. There is no one there to witness the cruelty. And about the hands, that is another matter entirely."

"Is it?" asked Lars. "Is cutting off a hand for failure to work any better or worse than flogging a man until he is nearly dead? In the end it is always about the same thing. It's always about money."

"My father says what the king does is important for our nation," said Benard, a well-to-do son of a manufacturing family. He leaned back in his chair and crossed his legs. "Our industry is improving and trade is stabilizing the economy.

"That is the way it has always been in England," Benard added.

"Historically nobility, or the landed class or those with titles, have been charged with the most important national decisions. Those who cannot even read or write are not worthy of a vote or a voice."

"In Louisiana, my people were not noble, and my great-grandmother was not even considered human by some. She was destined for bondage by nothing more than the color of her skin. Should she and her children have no vote and no voice either? There isn't as much difference between our nations as you think."

"But you can't compare black American slaves to these wild natives of the jungle."

"Aren't they the same? One group simply lives in Africa and speaks another language, but they are still human beings one and all. Here I am, educated just like you, and yet my grandmother was one of these 'cannibals.'"

Benard spoke up again tentatively, his words mimicking those of many Belgian industrialists. "But my father says they're children, and it's our duty to act as their parents, to take care of them."

"A good father doesn't sever his child's hand as punishment for an infraction. I do admit, some will flog their children, but even that is barbaric. The world is watching our king and his henchmen in Congo. Aren't you ashamed?"

Benard looked away, and it was clear he was struggling with what he knew was right and what his father insisted was for the good of the people.

"The British newspapers are particularly outspoken about the king's men there on the river and how it is the equivalent of enslaving a people without removing them from their homeland."

"Did you catch our professor's statement at the end of the lecture today?" Benard asked his friends.

"Ah, you mean his suggestion that the state must buy Congo from the king?"

"Yes. That's what Father says should be done."

"That's only because he wants a part of the profits instead of all of it going to the crown."

The young men laughed softly, for they all knew that money was the reason that Belgium was in Congo. It was a small European nation that needed the rubber and the mines and the bananas.

"Maybe so," Adrien said. "At least it would change everything down there if Belgian companies took over the trade. That would force king's agents out so a new system could be created. Unfortunately the damage is already done."

Adrien stirred his coffee and waited until he had his friends' attention. "My father said fate can sometimes place a man in a rare position where he has the power to affect a great deal of change. I believe we are in just such a position right now."

"To work for my father in Congo, Adrien, or something else?" Bernard offered.

"That's one way to fix it, but then again there will be money involved, and that will cause new problems that arise. Plus, they say the Indian plantations are near maturity, so the need for wild rubber will soon decline anyway."

Lars piped up. "Which means, Bernard, there will be no work for you there."

Again the men laughed at the futility of the entire venture, but Bernard raised his hand and continued. "Father speaks of diamonds and copper as well. Once the rubber mess is cleaned up, he talks about the Kasai to the south and its riches."

"And so the story begins again," Adrien said with a degree of sadness. "There's little doubt that in the end the people will suffer and the Belgians will grow rich without repairing the damage they caused in Equator Province. It is so remote and so many were murdered that thousands of children are crowding into the few missions upriver."

Lars smiled. "Ah, Hadriann, I see you have been listening to the Jesuits again."

"I admit, it's true. Two of them were at the university recruiting missionaries strong enough to survive the jungles and bring what's left of those people back to God."

This grisly 1904 photo shows two Congolese men holding dried, severed hands, used as currency among the agents of King Leopold II, who are shown flanking the Africans. Anyone failing to return from the jungle without meeting their quota of wild rubber sap would have their hand or that of a child promptly amputated unless they had the requisite number of dried hands to make up the difference.

"I suspect you, my friend, will follow your father's footsteps." Bernard said, reminding Adrien of his father's stories of changing the Confederate world into one that gave the colored class full civil rights. "And mark my words. I predict that Adrien will one day join the Jesuits."

❧

Adrien spoke often with Father Leon, the Jesuit missionary, about his eyewitness accounts of atrocities in the Congo. It made the young man recall how easily he and his brothers could pick out freed slaves on the streets of New Orleans. They never looked anyone in the eye, and a frightened, almost panicky aura surrounded every one. Should a white man or woman come out on the street at the same time or come in the opposite direction, these newly freed men and women would instantly cross the street or turn a corner to remain as far from them as they could.

Adrien felt the same restlessness in his own household when he was nine years old, during that difficult year of 1888 when his mother's family fought the Dejan brothers in open court. Here in Belgium, where his mother said equality reigned, he found a horror nearly as great as that of the slave-holding South. Somewhere along the way, Adrien began to feel deeply obliged to follow his father's path. But this time it would not be in the courts or the legislature. This time it would be in the name of his God.

Father Leon brought Adrien to a gathering of missionaries, and they discussed a single order of Belgians allowed unfettered access upriver in the Congo. Known as the Scheutists, they were centered in the small community of Scheut, Belgium. Officially named the Confraternity of the Immaculate Heart of Mary, CICM, this order was well known in Europe. While most other missionaries were at Louvain for a short time to preach in church or give speeches, the Scheutists seemed to always be around. Adrien came to know many of them who found his family's political history in colored New Orleans fascinating. Together they would enjoy many long discussions over the role of missionaries in world politics. Naturally he would learn a great deal about the history of Congo, the thousand tribes that lived along the great Zaire River, and their deep roots in the slave trade.

Though Adrien kept to his medical studies for his parent's sake, he gradually shifted to theology. Should they learn he had abandoned medicine, they might bring him home or force a change in schools. He would become friends with Romain Calbrecht, whose mother was a native of Scheut and dreamed of her youngest son joining the order. The two young men often spoke of motherly expectation and the possible impacts of the future announcement that Adrien would not become a physician but a missionary priest.

Romain was religious, but he was even more interested in politics. "The only way to do anything about the conditions in Congo is to join the

Scheutists. They have free access to all of it. The other missionary orders and a few Protestants are restricted to the coast and to Kasai, so they will never go near the rubber producing regions. Belgium would prefer the atrocities disappeared forever."

Adrien didn't share his theological interests with his family until graduation, when he wrote his mother he would take his degree in theology. This did not please her or Jean Benjamin at all when they read his letter saying he would not come back to New Orleans but move on to seminary under the Scheutists. He hoped they found some degree of relief, though, for Adrien was informed by his sisters' notes that the situation in Louisiana had gone from bad to worse.

After so long away from home, the tight-knit community of Scheutists became Adrien's new family. Both Romain and Adrien agreed to never reveal their feelings about repairing the wreckage caused by their king because some of the older Scheutists were still loyal to the monarchy. For them there was little separation between loyalty to their king and to their God. After much study Adrien finally made his final vows there in the Scheut motherhouse.

In theology school Adrien had begun to grow the great beard shared by missionaries in Africa. They say the beards were to better resemble God as illustrated in their catechisms and prayer books. Soon after holy orders, Adrien boarded ship to sail back to New Orleans for a brief rest prior to assignment to the missions. It had been nearly a decade since he had seen the city of his birth, and he would come home wearing his long black cassock and crucifix pinned to his chest.

Adrien did not find New Orleans much changed, but conversations with his father revealed the ugly truth. It seemed the light had gone out in Jean Benjamin's eyes—the man's bearing suggested defeat under the shadow of Jim Crow. Adrien was shocked by all the new restrictions both in the form of laws and of social etiquette. It was the latter that was enforced with nocturnal vigilante violence.

For Jean, it was difficult to explain the ugly details to his naïve son. "You must understand, Adrien, that even your cassock won't protect you from these people. Violating their rules has caused no end of suffering. Above all, if we meet anyone who is white, particularly a woman, don't be offended if she doesn't offer you her hand in friendship."

"How can shaking a hand become such a disrespectful act?"

"They couldn't win the war, so they are carefully re-creating our world on their terms." Jean Benjamin snipped off the end of his cigar and paused to light it. "At least before the war we lived by the law. Now it's these other codes, the ones that divide us from our white brothers, that seem to change every other day."

"So perhaps all that is necessary is to avoid them."

"That is the whole idea. You see, if we're always afraid, then we will simply stay away from them. That is what they want. It's becoming a segregated city, at least on the surface."

Adrien realized that white New Orleans now resembled the European nobility that Benard was always talking about. The equity sought during Reconstruction had faded into the past.

"So the white men no longer visit the women of Tremé?"

"Oh, there is no change there. They created Storyville, where it all may be done in secret. Out on the streets, the separation is real, but behind closed doors, things can be different. More and more restaurants and bars make us enter by separate doors, and if they serve colored people, we must dine in the kitchen."

Adrien's heavy brows came together as he walked down the banquette with his father, who nodded to passersby, but there were no longer the happy social greetings of his childhood. He could sense the ambient fear that was formerly restricted to the newly emancipated slaves. Now it was pervasive among the more elite colored community too.

"Where is it all going, Father?"

"We don't know. The other merchants I spoke with say that Mama Dejan was unwise building the house where she did because there are too many colored people living there. It never mattered before. There is talk of segregated neighborhoods."

"Just another way to keep us separated from them?"

"They hope so. The Democrats are drawing up a bill as we speak that will make it illegal for a colored man to buy a house in a white neighborhood. And likewise it will be illegal for a white to buy in a colored part of town like ours. That will make our property lose half its value if Dauphine and Barracks becomes officially colored."

"How can they enforce such a thing? Particularly when a family like ours has both white and colored under the same roof?"

Jean Benjamin shook his head sadly. "They are threatening to make the penalty a deterrent. Buying in the wrong neighborhood can result in forfeiture of your home or building. Can you believe they want to demolish or burn down the house if one should keep their family background secret? This is truly unconstitutional according to Judge Theard, and even he is growing fearful, dare I say discouraged, with the way things are going."

"Then perhaps it's better that I am going to the missions."

"It pains me to agree with you. I suspect even physicians will be legally restricted to serving only those of their own race as well. It is separation, pure and simple. Our people and their people will never occupy the same place."

"But theirs will run the world."

At the end of the week, Adrien climbed the pulpit of St. Augustine Church in his white vestments and read from Acts of the Apostles about tongues of fire and the start of Christian missions. Then he gave a stirring homily inspired by what he had seen in New Orleans. He spoke of the power of the Holy Spirit to help man continue to try even when he is knocked down by both his own sin and the prejudice of others. He preached of tenacity and of family, and the importance of retaining ties no matter how great the social and legal pressures.

Mama Dejan and the entire family filled the front pew for the Mass. Paul Filbert, Christine, and their sons traveled down from Baton Rouge, daring to sit in the whites-only rail car. The church was full of the religious from other parishes who came to see their native son's first Mass. There were many familiar faces in the pews, with the full range of skin tones from very dark to snowy white in the colored section. Although the Catholic churches became one of the few places that still allowed the mingling of races, those races were divided into different sections of the audience.

The Esnards had no idea of his plan for going to Africa, although his father had commented about articles in the *Tribune* about "nasty business" with the Belgians in Congo. When the time came to go, Adrien would

return to Scheut before sailing south to Boma, Congo's port on the Atlantic Coast. He had grown as fond of Jo and Flo and Marcel as he was his cousins in Europe, this time telling his own stories of life in the great Old World cities. Paul Filbert's three boys would miss their uncle the most, and all three cried outright as they waved their good-byes from the top of the levee. Adrien stood at the rail of the steamer as it pulled out into the river, his lean form a black pillar except for the tendrils of long black beard waving with the breeze.

Ordination photo of Adrien Benjamin Esnard, Belgium

PART IX

EXODUS

---- ⚜ ----

MAMA DEJAN

Dauphine Street, 1912

HE TURN OF THE CENTURY HAD BROUGHT THEM ONLY heartache. The statute had finally passed that would forever designate that corner of Barracks and Dauphine Streets as a colored neighborhood. Mama Dejan had watched the beauty of their community rapidly decline, the buildings growing derelict as many divested, the cross-town business fading. There was difficulty keeping sales at an even pace due to modern furniture manufacturing plants in newer parts of the city. More and more of their household income was derived from the interest from notes and mortgages, rentals and real estate profits. The family spent more time on the river as the demand for employees dwindled.

Mama Dejan was nearly eighty years old when an unusually cold winter struck New Orleans. The banana trees froze to the ground all across the Quarter, and in the mornings a thin sheet of ice covered the drainage ditches. The sickness began as a simple head cold, forcing Josephine to her bed, and the symptoms quickly progressed to pneumonia. Finally the priest from St. Augustine was called to confer the last rites. Jean Benjamin and Rene sat at Josephine's bedside as Florentine prepared the room for her inevitable passing. When Mama Dejan died, it rocked the family. She had been their strength through so many decades of war, social change, and political upheaval.

The extent of Mama Dejan's world was far greater than anyone knew. Her funeral mass had to be moved to St. Louis Cathedral because St. Augustine Church was far too small to accommodate it. The rite was attended by six priests, and the altar and casket were packed with flowers. Outside it rained, the sky crying to match the tears of her family and friends who took such strength from this ambitious woman. Many were inspired by her loyalty to Pierre and her efforts in the Dejan brothers suit to defend their union without shame.

In those days before World War I, New Orleans had become so incredibly hostile toward its colored community that her death seemed to represent all they had lost, that brief chance to gain civil rights crushed under the tightening noose of Jim Crow legislation. She became the metaphor for Marigny, which was declining into blight as business suffered under restrictive segregation. And white women like Mama Dejan who felt no shame in marrying a man of color would vanish under the pressure. With her would go the belief that all were equal, and that the mingling of the races could, in time, bring prosperity to them all.

This would be the most difficult year for Florentine. She had known for some time that Rene was flirting with disaster. He had graduated from Tulane Dental School as a bachelor and did not marry due to possible concerns for producing a colored child. Or perhaps he just never got around to getting married. When Mama Dejan died in 1912, he was twenty-eight.

Though he was a successful dentist in the Quarter, Rene was restricted to working exclusively for colored and black patients. He was legally prevented from such intimacies with whites. The social climate in the Quarter had become so restrictive for men of color that they began to visit the notorious Storyville district, where the rules of segregation were not so carefully enforced. This separate community of bars and brothels would offer the freedom for a new music to be born, called jazz, which blended the classical European training with the beat-driven tempo of Africa.

With no wife or children to form bearings in life, Rene was free to pursue women. It is no mystery how Rene's mysterious illness began, but it was never openly discussed. Syphilis was incurable, and death would come only after the disease entered the brain, leading to insanity. When Rene grew too sick, he was sent to a convalescent home in California for a cure. He returned to New Orleans somewhat improved and eager to share his great enthusiasm for the West Coast, where the issue of race seemed to be all but invisible. But by the day of Madame Dejan's funeral, he was again too ill to work. Yet he would marry a Chicago girl, Hazel, who gave him one son, Jack. In the end, Rene would be hospitalized in an asylum for the insane as syphilis invaded his brain. He died in 1929.

Marcel, the darling of his three older sisters, showed considerable drive to become a dentist like his brother Rene, whom he so admired. Florentine did not want Marcel to become unsettled for want of a wife as Rene had after graduating from Tulane Dental School, so she felt that he should study in the North where he stood a chance to live and marry as a white man. Marcel's relocation became part of the great migration of people of color fleeing the South for security and employment in northern cities. Black men and women went north for jobs in Chicago and other large urban areas, where they lived in enclaves such as New York's Harlem. Those light-complexion mixed-race families like the Esnards were able to start a whole new life as whites due to the widespread presence of swarthy Italians. Marcel, like Paul Filbert, could and did pass quite easily once fully separate from New Orleans and the common knowledge of the Esnard family. Marcel's daughter Lois would be the last child born to this generation, and one of only five offspring overall.

With the death of her mother, Florentine and her sister Pauline inherited their mother's entire estate, which was estimated at close to a million dollars by this time. Jean Benjamin became its full-time executor. With

In Florentine's later years, Adrienne would become the executor of the family investments, carrying on for her mother.

only the three adult daughters still at home, Raoul having left, the surviving Esnards came to a crossroads. There was no future for them in New Orleans. Though they were among the wealthier families in the city, all three daughters were effectively barred from society. Marriage to a colored man was out of the question. Taking a job was equally unsuitable, for none had the slightest bit of education or training. Despite the pale color of their skin, the well-known family name meant they could never look forward to employment opportunities above the level of a domestic. Adrienne, Flo, and Jo were doomed to live in the limbo of spinsterhood, isolated by a culture that would cloister their lives as effectively as antebellum plantations had controlled the lives of Africans that came before them.

❧

PAUL FILBERT ESNARD

Baton Rouge, 1913

W ITH THE PASSAGE OF EACH NEW STATUTE OF MISCE-
genation, Paul Filbert was assured he had made the right decision
to start life over again in Baton Rouge. His only reservation was if
he should have gone farther north than the state of Louisiana itself. Though
he and Christine lived as whites, there always remained the specter of discovery. Should word spread of their origins and, worse yet, the succession
trial, their whole world would be threatened and every choice questioned.
Theirs became a life carefully lived, one in which each act was prescribed to
maintain the status quo, and discussion of their relatives to the south was
forbidden.

If discovered, would they be pressured to move to another neighborhood
in a colored district? How many loyal customers would find another jeweler?
Could they become pariahs at
their church? Everyone they
knew who naturally considered them a white family could
suddenly turn away, angry and
vindictive at being so deceived.
Despite all of that, there was
still the criminal side of the
matter with its fines and penal-
ties and incarceration. Whether
legal or social, discovery would
force the Esnards back to the
other side of the fence.

Paul Filbert Esnard and Christine Brechtel's three sons
from left to right: John Adrien Esnard, Raoul Paul
Esnard, MD, and, on the right, Jean Benjamin Esnard II,
who would assume ownership of Esnard Jewelers in
Baton Rouge.

Perhaps most unique is that Paul Filbert took on this risk by having children. He would be the only one in his generation to marry and have more than one child. This young couple must have prayed that none of their offspring were so dark that they could possibly be dragged into colored life again. Fortunately the influx of Italians and other darker ethnicities into Louisiana was lessening the visibility of African blood, but in terms of offspring, there was no way to predict how the genes would manifest. While Marcel's daughter had no worries in New Jersey, his son Jack soon moved with his mother to California to escape New Orleans segregation.

Esnard Jewelers in downtown Baton Rouge had started up under Paul Filbert just as his grandfather Pierre did the furniture empire—by purchasing old pieces for resale. Many destitute white southerners were successful merchants and planters before the war. If there was one asset the family retained until the bitter end, it was their valuable jewelry. Cuff links, watches, earrings, rings, and broaches could be hidden away from the Yankees and later sold for taxes or simply to put food on the table. These heirlooms were often pawned in emergencies for a fraction of their real value, and the difference helped to make Esnard Jewelers as successful as Mama Dejan's furniture store.

Paul Filbert became an expert at buying old gold and his eye for gem quality was shared by his hawkeyed wife, Christine. She would become the driving force in this business—again, a white woman with her colored husband, but in this case it was unknown in the community at large. But it is certain that Paul Filbert and Christine knew the importance of keeping as much of their business as possible in her name to protect against race laws in the future.

When Paul Filbert was not at the engraver's bench, he was out on the golf course. The shop was left to Christine and their three sons, Jean Benjamin II, blue-eyed John Adrien, and Raoul Paul. The sons were raised in the business to become experts at the evaluation of old gems, learning from their mother how to determine age, clarity, and quality of the diamonds that once bejeweled the southern belles of antebellum times. All three were master engravers and became known for their decorated watches, which are still collected today.

It's not known how Flo met the successful doctor from Houston whose name was never known to the rest of the family. They fell desperately in love, so the story goes, and wished to marry. But that required Florentine's blessing. Because Florentine had so much power over her children, driven by their dependence on the family wealth, when she forbade her daughter from marrying the man, Flo obeyed. Florentine claimed this restriction was because her youngest daughter was destined to care for her in her old age, as was the tradition in a French family. However, with two other unmarried adult daughters, there was likely another, more secret reason. Color would again place a most difficult decision before these women, which ultimately forced Flo to leave the doctor because marriage without her mother's blessing was inconceivable. She would never fully recover because life offered little promise for the future.

There was no reason to remain in New Orleans after Mama Dejan's death, and Florentine was eager to visit California to see if it would be more beneficial for her chronic bronchitis than humid Louisiana. Moving would be no easy feat, for there was much property to dispose of, which would take time. So the Dauphine Street house went on the market, and the family began selling off the last of the furniture store inventory in preparation for closing the store.

Jean Benjamin had great difficulty coping with the change. While the city of his birth was no longer the same place, he didn't want to leave the remnants of his extended family. It was his home. He knew every inch of the Quarter, and nearly everyone who lived there recognized him as an icon. Moving so far away to an unknown city meant severing his ties with everything familiar. He smoked incessantly and spent more time playing chess when not contending with the avalanche of paperwork. Florentine had banished him to the porch to protect her frail lungs.

It struck him most acutely when they sold the family burial tomb, which stood in St. Louis Cemetery #3, square 2-D, no. 15. There lay Simeon and Marie Louise Smith. The remains of Etienne and Marie Felix may have also rested there. This tomb, this bit of ground in that walled old cemetery, was his touchstone to life before the war, to the beautiful culture that he loved so deeply. To sell the tomb would be like betraying them, but when it was gone, he would be free of the sadness that haunted him since the Great Compromise of 1877. He and all the others who had fought for their civil rights after the war had their constitution gradually washed away. Their rights vanished like the clay banks along the Mississippi—they were hard as rock in the dry season, but many years of high water gradually wore them down to nothing more than the suggestion of elevation in the floodplain.

This is the Esnard family tomb, sold upon their departure from New Orleans.

ADRIEN BENJAMIN ESNARD

Boyange St. Paul, Belgian Congo, 1915

WHEN ADRIEN DISEMBARKED AT BOMA, THE PORT city of the Congo at the delta of the great river Zaire, he felt as though he was home again. The dominance of both a powerful muddy river and the coastal moisture recalled all those steamy summers on the River Road. Like New Orleans, the port was busy with thousands of black faces loading and unloading the ships. He was among the few pale ones in the crowd that whirled with brilliant fabrics like the parades of Mardi Gras. It was home in all but the language.

A Congolese acolyte met him at the ship, and they walked through the streets to a small building owned by the missionaries who handled all their overseas transit. From there he boarded a train that wound its way on enormous yet precarious trestles up the massive escarpment from which the river

This photo from the CICM archives shows Adrien and his fellow Scheut missionaries onboard the ship to Congo. Adrien is the sixth man from the right, shown here without a hat.

tumbled in extraordinary cataracts of white spray and mist. It pulled into Leopoldville across from a widening in the river. Here the water slowed and broad spans of water lilies spread out from the shoreline. Floating rafts of debris accumulated over a thousand miles made their way toward the falls.

At the motherhouse in Leopoldville, Adrien began

his African education. With other new conferees of Scheut, he slowly adjusted to the tropical African climate. Even more trying was to learn Lingala, a single tongue invented by the Belgians to unify the hundred different tribal languages upriver. When not in the classes, Adrien spent a great deal of time in the fields of banana trees and other crops, preparing to grow them at his future mission. If he were to create a community far into the interior, they would require self-sufficiency, and should the mission manage a crop to sell, it would provide valuable income for expansion.

This is the earliest photo of Adrien in the Congo during his brief stay before CICM moved him to the Philippines to help the Belgians make inroads with the American officials after the Spanish-American War. He would be back in Africa within a year.

Each day, Adrien waited to learn his assignment, but none came. Then the Superior General sent for him. He eagerly arrived in anticipation of the news.

"You're our only American, as you well know, Adrien. And of course you speak English, and that is what we need the most right now. Now that the Americans' war with Spain is over, there's a need for a liaison between our missionaries and the occupational government in Philippines. They are Americans, naturally."

"But Superior General, I prepared for Africa. There is important work to do there."

"Hundreds of thousands have died in the Philippines, Adrien. You're essential to our establishment of new missions there at this critical time. Certainly you understand. I believe our Lord sent you to us for just this opportunity."

"I don't speak the Philippine language or Spanish."

"That may be true, but your value to us is in helping with the Americans in particular. There's no question they are predisposed to the Protestant missions. For us to gain a solid foothold there, we must cultivate a relationship with them."

"With the bureaucrats, eh?"

"Ah, I forgot. Didn't you say your father was somewhat political?"

"He left office long before I was born. But I suppose to live in New Orleans is to live with its everyday political realities."

"Then you are our man, Adrien. The ship leaves in a week, then you shall meet with Father Detrickx as superior, and travel to the Philippines with eight others. Your work with the Americans is just as important as winning souls. It must be done so we may bring more souls to God. As much as we disdain politics, it has always been woven into the mission life."

✤

When the steamer docked in Manila, Adrien set out to help his small group get settled in the islands under the new American regime. The Scheutists hoped to gain access to a sizeable field in the interior, but it was pending official permission.

Still a citizen of the United States, Adrien carried his documents in hand when visiting the customs office to discuss visas for his brothers from CICM. Those managing the port were military men in their drab olive uniforms and campaign hats. One man studied Adrien's paperwork then handed it to another beside him to read, then looked back at Adrien. There was a curious look on the man's face.

"Y'all's from Louisiana," the officer said as he shuffled the papers on his desk. The noticeable southern drawl was all too familiar to Adrien, who remained stoic. "We got a whole lot of trouble brewing around here with them Creoles. You a Creole, boy?"

As always, the meaning of that word was ambiguous. To some it meant the descendants of French or Spanish settlers. To others, it meant those whose white blood mingled with that of Africans.

"Depends on how you define Creole, monsieur," Adrien replied politely. "I've been living in Belgium for the past eight years. My city of origin is not relevant here."

"Oh, but I think it is. Could be them Papists is using you to get the Creoles all stirred up again around here. Maybe you want to see them control this country again. Well, that ain't gonna happen. And I think you's a Creole because I can smell 'em. It's just natural with me. Maybe the other fellas got to see for themselves, but I know already."

Adrien didn't respond. He knew there was nothing he could say to change the man's clear bias.

The other official looked up from Adrien's papers and smiled. "Esnard, you will have to shave that beard if you want into the Philippines. We need to know exactly who you are. It's orders from the general."

Adrien knew instinctively what was happening, and he could feel the hair rising on the back of his neck. He'd seen the same attitude among the men his father had branded Confederates-turned-Democrats back home. He'd forgotten how demeaning they could be without saying anything overtly discriminatory. This was the root of his innate distrust of anyone exhibiting too much of a mannerly way, for that was how southerners often disguised their derisive tone.

The young priest was mature now, and his facial features were more distinctly African due to the Congo sun. Shaving would remove all doubt about his origins, and like his father, he had planned to cover those sensuous lips for the rest of his life. But now he was forced to bear his face to these men, which he would do as a sign of humility and subordination to his work with CICM. For them he would make a sacrifice and open himself to scrutiny.

Father Detrickx himself watched as Adrien shaved for the first time in many years. The upper half of his face was darkened by the sun, but the lower half was far more pale. Without his beard, Adrien felt exposed and vulnerable, not among the missionary brothers but each time he went out in public. He realized that some of the soldiers had come from the South, which had been economically depressed since the Civil War. They left many hardscrabble farms or disintegrating towns to find security and income in the armed forces

It was not long before two letters arrived at the office of the Superior General in Belgium on the same day:

Manila October 30, 1908

To the Reverend Father Superior General;

I have hardly arrived in Manila and I am traveling again, not to the interior of the country, but to Shanghai to await your orders. The Apostolic Delegate informed Fr. Detrickx that I am not the person they need for the Philippines . . . I can't write you the condition in which my soul finds itself at this moment . . . It had to be quite worthwhile to be called from the deep interior of the Congo. May the holy will of God be done. I am leaving tomorrow for Hong Kong where I will await the boat from Shanghai. —A. Esnard

Manila October 30, 1908

Terrible news! They refuse Fr. Esnard because he is a "mestizo negro." Here are the facts in all their brutality. As motives, the Americans are against them, bordering to superstition. Even the bishop and Archbishop as was attested by the laypersons and all the priests I have seen. Wherever he would work here he would have the opposition of the local American. With his beard I wouldn't even have suspected that Fr. Esnard is black—without it he is beautiful and well a "negro." I don't want to send him back to Belgium, so I send him to Shanghai until further decisions from Scheut. —Fr. Detrickx

Scheut chose to send Adrien back to Africa. There was no question that Adrien had met with serious disagreements with the Americans, and the Belgians learned for the first time just how deep the roots of racism ran in the South. Perhaps they felt sympathy that he was rejected by his own people, and they hoped this man of color might find redemption and the peace he deserved at a remote mission station.

So upon returning to Leopoldville, Adrien would be assigned to Equateur Province as a traveling priest, visiting villages and outposts not yet developed enough for a mission. For months on end he would travel with his bearers through the equatorial rain forests of Congo far from that single linking artery, the River Zaire; its fleet of riverboats served the many Belgian colonial ports along the river, first created for the rubber and ivory trade.

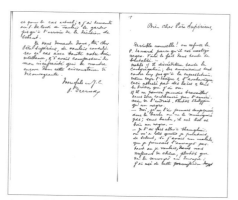

A copy of the original letter describing Adrien's experience with Americans in Manila.

Traveling in Congo jungles was not easy. Only the young strong priests were given this task of visiting the villages to give the sacraments and preach to the people. Adrien's unique ability to survive tropical diseases kept him strong and vigorous, traveling with his trusted Mauser rifle that not only offered protection but also fresh meat.

Finally his superiors decided that Adrien had grown accustomed to the jungle. They offered him the most remote region, deep in the interior. The port was Lisala, located a thousand miles inland from the coast. It was the homeland of the Budjala, and Scheut charged Adrien with the job of establishing a mission to convert and educate them. It would be named Boyange St. Paul Mission.

This map of Africa provided by the Belgian missionaries shows the location of Lisala's port with a simple *LI* next to the region north of there where Adrien founded Boyange St. Paul.

This rare photo at Boyange St. Paul shows Adrien seated at right. With his beard, longer hair, and skin darkened by the equatorial sun, he resembles an Australian Aborigine compared to the Europeans.

Hacking a plantation out of the jungle was no small task, and building anything in such a climate so far from the river was next to impossible. Adrien would struggle to establish the most important part of the mission: a church. His first church simply collapsed. The second one, made of thatch, burned to the ground. Then the third effort followed much later after they created a brick kiln and made bricks out of the dense Congo clay. It stood out in the rugged landscape, European in design and as large as St. Augustine's in New Orleans.

From there the Budjala slowly built an enormous mission station led by Adrien's boundless strength and dedication. His people would dub him *Yeye Mobali*, which, strictly translated, means "man of men." Perhaps it was the unusual American priest's love of the hunt or instincts honed by Mississippi delta agriculture that made his mission so productive that the Scheutists asked that its largesse be used to feed the entire vicariate with its proceeds. Also from the old South were the Negro spirituals, which Adrien knew well and which he taught to the Budjala. Their rich voices and harmonies brought back memories of childhood masses at St. Augustine.

Unlike his European-born brothers, Adrien did not fall ill often. Africa was rife with tropical diseases from malaria to blackwater fever. Aside from an occasional "rest cure" to Belgium, Adrien would not suffer like other Scheutists in Congo. It's likely he obtained immunity from diseases experienced as a child in steamy New Orleans, which provided antibodies to the same afflictions in equatorial Africa. For the Africans, sickle-cell genes are believed to be responsible for resistance to malaria, one of the most widespread killers. Such genes could have been the factor that protected

The third and final church built at Boyange St. Paul.

XXXVᵉ Année. Nᵒ 10. Octobre 1927.

Missions de Scheut

Revue Mensuelle — Cette revue paraît le 15 de chaque mois
— Abonnements : Belgique : 10.00 fr. — Union postale : 4 Belgas. —
Adresse
Missionnaires de Scheut, Chaussée de Ninove, 476, Bruxelles
— Administration : R. P. BOSMAN, (Compte chèque 33.776) —

SOMMAIRE : Une grave nouvelle : meurtre d'un missionnaire. — Les Origines
de la Congrégation de Scheut (suite). — Nécrologe.

CONGO. La mission de Boyange.
(Vicariat de Nouvelle-Anvers).
C'est une des plus jolies missions de tout le Congo, située au milieu de

A rare example of the expansive European-style gardens at Boyange St. Paul is displayed on the cover of the newsletter *Missions de Scheut.*

Adrien from this common scourge.

Adrien had finally found his place in the world at Boyange, and there he expressed great joy in his accomplishments. He would live and hunt with his people because Adrien was no longer afraid of growing darker under the sun. He was the superior of Boyange St. Paul, and that was indisputable, even if he more resembled one of the Budjala than a Belgian missionary.

Somehow, Adrien's work in Africa seemed to close a circle that had been unresolved for so many generations. He would surround himself with the dark-skinned people of his childhood home, so familiar and yet so different. They would never question his race and therefore his right to be a free man. Adrien often sat upon the shaded balcony of the priest's house at Boyange and looked out on its extensive gardens. It felt so familiar, just like those days at Cazillard watching the setting sun glint upon the wide Mississippi.

There is no question that Adrien felt a kinship with his people, though his view of the Budjala was probably more paternally European. Perhaps that is why they were so willing to create such an extraordinary community at Boyange. As superior, Adrien's letters and reports described growth through numbers, recording the growing number of baptisms and the education of Budja catechists to extend his world deeper into Equateur.

The most frequent requests later on were for supplies and medicine, but subtly included was a carefully worded plea for more ammunition. Leopards hunted in the dark of night, and these big cats were dangerous around a mission due to the number of children gathered there for education. Ammunition would allow Adrien to hunt down a dangerous cat, but he had no ammunition and hunted with the Budja men using spears. He had any leopard pelts tanned and sent them home to his parents and siblings, some of which pelts are still in the family.

ADRIENNE ESNARD

ELDEST DAUGHTER OF JEAN BENJAMIN AND FLORENTINE

Raymond Street, Los Angeles, 1913

DRIENNE, FLORENTINE'S OLDEST DAUGHTER, WAS A raving beauty with an irrepressible personality just like her mother and grandmother. She yearned for release from the increasingly claustrophobic social milieu of the French Quarter and what was becoming a segregated neighborhood. The Esnards first rented a home in Long Beach, which to the girls seemed like heaven. Now Adrienne could go anywhere she wished and speak to anyone and about any topic without fear they might discover her colored family history. She was now just Adrienne Esnard, big sister of Jo and Flo.

The move was not so easy for Jean Benjamin. This third-generation native of New Orleans was a son of the South and fit perfectly into the genteel colored community. He missed the urban Quarter desperately, for in Los Angeles there was no place to gather, no curbside cafes, no jazz, no beignets, and, above all, no chess. He found this new life dull and colorless despite the beautiful homes and gardens, all fantastically new compared to centuries-old Vieux Carre townhomes with their peeling paint and rusting cast iron. He even missed the smell of mildew and despaired at never hearing another person speak French outside his new house.

This family photo was taken during Adrien's visit home after his father passed away before World War II. In this photo at the Raymond Street house, left to right in the front row are Flo and Jo; back row is Adrien, Florentine, and Adrienne with Mr. Bill.

139

Each time Jean felt himself descending into the lonely darkness, when the loss of his deeply familiar lifestyle became too much to bear, he would light a new cigar and count his blessings. Then he'd close his eyes and remember as the nicotine soothed him. Jean Benjamin missed the hustle-bustle of the Quarter, the foot traffic and voices filled with patois and deep drawl. There was no clip-clop of horse-drawn vendors. Instead, shiny automobiles traveled quietly down broad, newly paved streets. Virtually no one was out and about on foot, and even fewer sat out on their porches. Most of all Jean missed the river, that great green ribbon that divided the old city of his youth. The rise and fall of that river set the seasons of trade. Gangs of stevedores on the levee brought excitement every day. And the bayous that fanned out from its banks became like deep roots of a tree that sheltered the city he loved.

In Los Angeles, Jean had no friends, and in his seventies he dutifully attended Mass on Sunday, while Florentine and her three middle-aged spinster daughters often went to daily Mass too. All that remained of Jean's old life was evenings on the porch drinking his Chambourg and smoking one cigar after another, leaving the woodwork forever reeking of tobacco. Florentine blamed his perpetual smoking for his asthma that developed after moving to Los Angeles. It became life threatening after Rene died and the stock market tumbled in 1929 to destroy many of their investments. At eighty-three he was otherwise quite healthy, the famous bristly mustache now snow white, but still thick enough to hide his luxuriant lips.

After a brief trip to the California desert to try to clear up the lung congestion, Jean came back to Raymond Street in 1930. It was late May, and the gardens were lush with roses and passionflower. Paul Filbert's youngest son, Raoul Paul, was living nearby with his wife, Benita, and their son, Little Paul. Raoul Paul had recently graduated from medical school and had come to help Jean to Sunday Mass along with his aunts and grandmother, who had grown quite frail in her old age. All was well that day when they breakfasted together, drinking strong French coffee while sitting with Jean out on the porch as he savored his one cigar for the day, having cut back due to his respiratory condition. Late that night, Jean Benjamin suffered a stroke. He was paralyzed and lingered for eight days at home until he finally died. It was just four days before their fifty-seventh wedding anniversary.

Adrien was notified of his father's illness and was summoned from Africa, but Jean died before the missionary arrived. Upon his return to the family, Adrien was thinner, his beard now short and mostly gray. He wore spectacles all the time and had lost the last two fingers of one hand to a tropical infection.

Though Adrien was thrilled to finally be reunited with his family, he was no longer superior at Boyange St. Paul Mission and missed it terribly. With such great success with his first mission, Scheut had allowed him to remain there for decades, a rare scenario for missionaries. Missionaries were not to become too attached to one place as Adrien had. Or perhaps there was another man who wished to take over the successful mission for himself. Oddly enough, his very success caused Scheut to teach him the value of humility by reassigning Adrien to mission Mbaya to the west. Mbaya was a complete disaster, its church unfinished and no other buildings to speak of. It would be starting all over again, and Adrien was now, by African terms, a very old man.

The Mbaya Mission that Adrien found was in total disarray, but in time it would become far more prosperous, as shown by this later CICM photo.

In the 1930 photos taken during the visit to Los Angeles, Adrien refuses to look at the camera. The sternness in his aged mother's face may have been grief or, as the photo suggests, a reflection of her general unhappiness in Los Angeles.

In letters written on his journey home through the Panama Canal to Los Angeles, Adrien would state in rather resentful terms that he would make no effort to raise money for the missions. His tone of voice was no longer jubilant, and the number of baptisms was no longer an accomplishment. Now he was depressed and saddened that he had been ripped away from his people, and he no doubt wondered if that was how his father had felt when the Great Compromise had suddenly cut off his own future in Louisiana government.

Adrien returned to Africa. All the missions would soon face privations during World War II when Belgium was invaded by the Nazis, and the flow of goods from Europe slowed to a trickle. Ammunition, medicine, vitamins, and oil were impossible to obtain. Even the mail system was not reliable.

Adrien survived the war years, though he suffered from internal parasites. He was stricken with a liver disease in 1947 and was moved to the missionary hospital in Leopoldville. There he soon passed away. He is buried in the Scheut cemetery in Leopoldville, the city renamed Kinshasa after its independence from Belgium in 1960.

This is a contemporary photograph of Adrien's grave at the end of the twentieth century in the city of Kinsasha, Congo, formerly known as Leopoldville.

This is a copy of the handwritten will of Adrien Esnard, written in the hospital before he passed away.

Soon after Adrien's visit to Los Angeles, his mother died. They all knew that she could not survive long without Jean Benjamin, and they were right. She was buried beside her husband in a Catholic cemetery in Los Angeles. Unlike her mother's large funeral in New Orleans, the services for Jean Benjamin and Florentine were attended by only a few family members because their new home had cut them off from a lifetime of relatives, friends, and neighbors who would have flocked to Jean's and Florentine's memorial.

The three Esnard women retained ownership of the Raymond house. Flo did what she believed was right and never married, even after the death of her mother. I would know her in her eighties, sweet and kind with her lace-up shoes identical to those of the nuns who taught our classes. She would visit us wearing heavy hose, big hats, and old-fashioned clothing. I believe this was the outside of a woman who had never really lived, remaining cloistered by race from birth. Relatives say Flo spent so much time lying

This photo shows Aunt Florentine in her lace-up shoes and formal attire with the author's siblings. Author is on far right.

down that her father dubbed her "Sister Recline." However cute they considered this moniker, it was in fact a tragic sign of depression.

The only daughter to marry was Adrienne, but only when she was well past menopause. When about sixty, Adrienne married a devout widower, Mr. Bill, whom she had met at Mass. They immediately began to travel, often bringing Flo and Jo with them on various trips. They joined Flo on a four-thousand-mile road trip all over the western United States, which helped her depression considerably. Mr. Bill died in 1945, leaving Adrienne alone once more. Together the Esnard women again traveled on the Cunard Line ship *Britannia* to see their family homeland and Biche relatives in France.

All of this traveling followed lifetimes without lovers, marriage, or children. After the death of Adrienne, Flo and Jo sold the Raymond Street house and bought their own smaller bungalow. By this time, they held the vast majority of the family wealth and were never wanting. However, they remained quite economical, living piously with few luxuries, like a pair of aged Catholic nuns. Flo outlived them all and died in 1970, her considerable fortune divided among the two children of her brothers, Rene and Marcel.

The Esnard women in Los Angeles. From left is Josephine, Adrienne, Florentine Krach Esnard, and Florentine.

RAOUL PAUL ESNARD, MD

Los Angeles

ARK-HAIRED AND CHARISMATIC, PAUL FILBERT'S SON, Raoul Paul, would become infamously linked to a female golf pro while still a teen in Baton Rouge. He eloped with her, but this was brief. His mother, Christine, was so incensed that she immediately went to the courts demanding the marriage be unceremoniously annulled. Then she put the boy on the train to Los Angeles to live with his grandmother and spinster aunts until the community gossip finally settled down. She hoped that Jean Benjamin would be able to put some sense into this boy's handsome head.

Next door to the Esnard's Raymond Street house was the home of Dwight Bennett Barnes, a lawyer from Delavan, Wisconsin. He had come out to California for health reasons with his wife, Alice, their son, Bennett, and daughter, Cornelia Benita, to enjoy the mild climate. Benita was thrilled to find a rakish young fellow had moved in with the Esnard women next door. His dark eyes, raven hair, and quick wit were beguiling.

Before anyone knew what was happening, Raoul eloped yet again, this time with lithe Benita, in a Model T, which they drove to Texas, where they were summarily married. They finally returned to Los Angeles after a passionate on-the-road honeymoon to face Bennett Barns. The lawyer made it clear that he expected

Raoul Paul Esnard, son of Paul Filbert, as a boy at his confirmation in Baton Rouge.

144

Marriage portrait of Raoul Paul Esnard of Baton Rouge and Cornelia Benita Barnes of Delavan, Wisconsin, after they eloped from Los Angeles to Texas.

A portrait of Raoul Esnard, MD, after graduating from medical school in St. Louis and returning to his wife and newborn son in Los Angeles.

this rakish young man from Louisiana to support his daughter in the way she was accustomed.

Barnes discovered Raoul Paul had the manual dexterity and the desire to become a physician, but his mother in Baton Rouge had forbidden medical school to force him to work at Esnard Jewelers. His romantic style and salesmanship sold more than his two brothers combined. For the good of his daughter, Bennett put up the money for Raoul Paul to attend UCLA and then the University of St. Louis School of Medicine in Missouri. While he was away in St. Louis, Little Paul was born.

Raoul Paul returned to Los Angeles, diploma in hand, to begin the arduous task of building a medical practice. He worked in the Jewish neighborhoods along Wilshire Boulevard close to where his young family lived in a Spanish-style bungalow on Gardener Street. Raoul Paul became a successful surgeon, growing his own fortune as he dedicated himself to a surging patient load in that thriving city. Late in life they built a large custom home on Rimpau Street in the Hancock Park area of Los Angeles.

During World War II, Little Paul was drafted to fly transport planes in the Air Corps. The doctor had always thought Little Paul would follow him into medicine and one day take over his thriving practice, but the boy lacked the desire and aptitude to become a medical doctor. Instead, Raoul Paul's daughter, Mary Alice, who spent summers working in her father's office, would become a psychologist, and her two daughters, nurses. Little Paul followed Bennett Barnes's lead and became an attorney. At school he met Audrey Hemphill and then graduated and worked in the Los Angeles District Attorney's office. They married and had six children and raised them in the San Fernando Valley.

PART X

PRESENT DAY

There probably exists in the mental life of the individual not only what he has experienced himself, but an archaic heritage. . . . The archaic heritage includes not only dispositions, but also ideational contents, memory traces of the experience of former generations.

—Sigmund Freud, *Moses and Monotheism*

MAUREEN ESNARD GILMER

Dobbins, California, 1990

M Y GRANDFATHER, RAOUL PAUL ESNARD, MD, DIED IN
1970 while I was still a young girl. He and my great-uncle Adrien were
the two sons of Paul Filbert, who immigrated from New Orleans to live
in Los Angeles. They knew their maiden aunts and grandparents while they
lived at the Raymond Street house and later when the girls moved to their own
house. The brothers left their third sibling, Jean Benjamin II, behind in Baton
Rouge to assume management of the jewelry store there. Other than these
three Esnard men, only two others were born to this lost generation. Marcel
had one daughter, Lois. Rene, who died prematurely, had one son, Jack, who
would also become a military surgeon. These were the sum total of that once
very large clan that grew up together in New Orleans. And there was even less
known about the forces that divided them.

A military photo of Little Paul during
World War II.

My grandmother Benita grew up
admiring her own aunt, a flapper who
smoked cigarettes, which was quite a
scandal in her day. Benita was quite open-
minded and had once told me her husband "came from an old Creole family."
My father always believed that meant
they were descendants of French immigrants, but he knew nothing more about
his grandparents' lives on Dauphine
Street. The move to Los Angeles had not
only boosted this group over the fence,
but they also virtually eliminated the

148

fence altogether within their own family by never recalling those days and struggles against racism in Louisiana.

About a decade after the passing of Raoul Paul, Benita died at the end of a long and difficult battle with emphysema. I spent a great deal of time with her as a child and often prowled the great dark attic of the Rimpau Street house, reading surgery books I found there and exploring my grandfather's fabulous handgun collection. She and I shared a special bond that continued beyond her passing, and her place in my life was filled with a relationship with her oldest daughter, Mary Alice. From Mary would come one of the few stories that testified to my grandfather's unusual relationship with African-Americans.

Raoul Paul the surgeon with one of this thoroughbred race horses in southern California.

Benita and Raoul Paul hired a black housekeeper, Ethyl, whom I personally remember. I recall Dad saying that my grandfather and Ethyl hated each other. They were always arguing, and their conflicts could raise quite a fit of temper. According to Mary Alice, who lived at home at the time, Ethyl became sick and called the doctor's office for an immediate appointment, as it was quite serious. Not realizing who she was, the nurses likely heard the Negro tone of her voice and would not put her through to the doctor nor make an appointment. They said that the doctor was booked up and she should seek another physician. Ethyl then called Benita, who immediately informed her husband. Raoul sent an ambulance to Ethyl's home that morning, and he was waiting for her at the hospital ER when she arrived. He diagnosed her as suffering from syphilis, which had invaded her reproductive organs. He performed the lifesaving surgery personally.

Ethyl was very sick, and for weeks Raoul Paul spent his lunch breaks hand-feeding her. He cared for her intimately and did not take a penny for his services. After she became well enough, she came back to their house and continued where she left off as housekeeper. Mary Alice believes this was a testament to his sensitivity to the often poor care given those of African American origin, particularly then in the 1950s. How much of that sensitivity was learned in Baton Rouge or New Orleans can only be verified by a comment by Benita, who said that when they briefly lived in Louisiana after their marriage, she "saw Negroes gunned down in the streets."

ANDRE LEBERT

Sur Sein, France, 1985

NDRE LEBERT WAS ABOUT EIGHTY WHEN I FIRST BEGAN to write him letters in France. He had long been interested in the American branch of his family and had sent an incomplete genealogy to my father years before to flesh out our side. My dad filled in what he knew, but that was very little, and then sent it back. So naturally this man would be the best place to start my inquiries about Adrien.

Andre, I would learn, was quite deaf but wrote fluently in English, French, and Arabic. He joined the Foreign Service and became a minister of civil servants in colonial French Algiers and lived there for a long time during the 1930s, when Adrien was in the Congo. He retired to Paris around World War II and was made a Knight of Malta by the French government. My search would create a lively correspondence between the two of us, with this old man who could communicate by pen so beautifully in his all-too-silent world.

Andre Lebert in Algiers while serving as French minister of civil service in the colony.

Andre would become my touchstone and rudder throughout this process, for he knew Adrien as a young man. It was with Andre that Adrien spent holidays while away at school in Belgium. He would become quite close with his cousins Andre and François, their parents, and grandparents. Even while Adrien was in Africa at the same time as Andre was in

150

Algiers, the men corresponded and often met in Europe when Adrien came home for a "rest cure" or on administrative business for his mission. Europeans who did not fare well in the equatorial African climate with its parasites and diseases often required the "rest cure." The need to return to Europe for physical as well as psychological recuperation was vital to their survival.

This scenario also taught me that few European missionaries survived more than twenty years in the African missions, particularly the most remote ones like Boyange. But Adrien lived forty-two years in the Congo, somehow managing to survive not only the ravages of malaria but blackwater fever, typhus, and a host of other fatal diseases. It is interesting to note that the first case of the dreaded hemorrhagic fever, Ebola Zaire, was discovered just a few miles from the Boyange mission.

My queries would bring Andre back to his own files on the American branch of the family and in particular the photos, letters, and other paraphernalia from his cousin in the Congo. He sent it all to me, handing off his life's work to learn more about the American side of the family. Together, thousands of miles apart, he and I would begin our twenty-year relationship to learn why Adrien went to school in Belgium while the rest of his siblings stayed at home, and even more curious, why he went to Africa at all.

CHRISTINE ESNARD METOYER

Long Beach, California, 1997

NOTHER OF PAUL FILBERT'S SONS, JOHN ADRIEN THE
dentist, was my godfather. He was among the most charismatic men
I have ever known, and to this day I recall his gold fillings glinting
beneath baby-blue eyes whenever he smiled. Big Adrien, as he was known to
differentiate from his son Little Adrien, lived in Orange County on Balboa
Island with his wife, Jeannette. He would pass away in 1988, and about a
decade later, Jeanette followed him, leaving her estate to be sorted out by her
oldest daughter, Christine Esnard Metoyer.

Christine was a controversial character in our family because she married
a black man. I had seen her only once in my life, in the limousine at my grandfather's funeral. Frankly, I'd never known she'd existed before that sad day.

In my Adrien quest, I called her after her mother's, Jeanette's, death
to ask that she keep an
eye out for anything in
her parents' papers that
might relate to Father
Adrien the missionary
or to the New Orleans
Esnards in general.
Christine told me that
her father was interested
in the priest and knew
there were some things
in the house. She said
there was a book with

Christine Esnard and her husband, James Metoyer, present day.

152

information on his life that I should see before I went any further and offered to send me their copy to look at.

When *God's Men of Color* arrived from Christine, I was thrilled to finally make progress because research was painfully slow and difficult before the advent of the Internet. The author was Father Albert S. Foley, an American Jesuit who wrote this controversial book in 1955 as the Civil Rights Movement in Louisiana was near the boiling point. The goal was to show the contributions of colored priests in American history.

Foley titled Adrien's chapter "*Ye Ye Mobali:* A Real He Man," proving that without question it was known that this priest was African-American. When I brought it up to my father, he was quite disturbed about the whole matter and wrote it off as a mistake in the Jesuit's research. Naturally such a response would offer a writer even more encouragement to learn the truth about the "mistake."

Foley had interviewed Adrien's youngest brother, Marcel, in New Jersey about Father Adrien's early life. It was here that I learned for the first time that Adrien was colored, and that the whole Esnard clan must have been more than just "an old Creole family," and were indeed of mixed race.

Also in Christine's generous package were original letters, some in English, others in French, written in Adrien's flawless penmanship to his family and a particularly beautiful one to Big Adrien, my godfather, the dentist. It was in English, and on the occasion of his marriage to Jeanette, Adrien expresses his pain at not being able to perform the ceremony himself.

Clearly Father Adrien knew my godfather as his namesake, having corresponded with him from the mission Mbaya. And I would realize that Uncle Adrien had to have known about the mixed-race ancestry, and as a result, so did my grandfather Raoul Paul. And yet they kept it from Little Paul, or perhaps it had become so irrelevant in California that there was no need to burden another generation with racial ghosts of the past.

NESTOR PYCKE, CICM

Rome, Italy, 1995

F ATHER FOLEY'S CHAPTER WAS THE KEY TO UNDER-
standing Father Adrien's strange choice of a Belgian missionary order.
After much research, I learned he had joined the Missionaries of the
Immaculate Heart of Mary, a rather obscure group with only one other non-
Belgian member, a Canadian. When Adrien was in school at Sint Niklaas
Diocesan College, he became close with Romain and Joseph Calbrecht, and
together all would be ordained through CICM. Adrien would remain to this
day the only American and the only African-American to join this European
order.

My letters of inquiry were sent to Kinshasa, then Belgium, and finally to
the archivist, Nestor Pycke, CICM. His work oversaw the incredible archive
and library at their new motherhouse in Rome, probably moved there for a
climate more amenable to the aging missionaries. It was just outside the city
at the end of a wild cab ride through the hills of Rome, where the priests lived
in a compound of buildings with a small order of nuns.

CICM had moved all their African archives to this new location, and
while there I saw students hard at work on ethnographic studies from the
earliest writings about the Congolese tribes as they were when first encoun-
tering Europeans. CICM's efforts to document the various groups helped
to found the missions and remains valuable data into African history for
modern researchers. Pycke took a personal interest in Adrien, who was fea-
tured in the fourth anniversary issue of *Missionhurst*, published in 1986.
In this article there was a CICM approach to his life and work that would
shed even more light on his life in the Belgian Congo and problems in the
Philippines.

Pycke began culling the substantial records for Boyange Mission and copied nearly every progress report Adrien wrote to his superiors in Leopoldville. All were in French, and Andre Lebert, who was then about ninety, translated many for me. This would begin a long series of correspondences between me and Father Pycke, who would send me data each time he came upon a new bit of information about Adrien or his missions. Pycke would copy what he could and send it to me in California. This is where I learned how vital it was to report the numbers of baptisms and catechists and the yields from Boyange's fertile fields. Among the records were photos depicting this man at his mission when he indeed resembled an Australian Aborigine.

Father Pycke would fill my files with these letters, which included Adrien's requests for ammunition and his enjoyment of a "motorcyclette," upon which he could get around the expansive mission far more quickly. I also received Adrien's personal articles to the order's newsletters published in Flemish Dutch. CICM proved one of the most beautiful discoveries of this entire project, for these highly educated men tempered in the world's most difficult climates were a pleasure to know.

COLLEEN FITZPATRICK

Garden Grove, California, 1990

HE INTERNET SPED UP MY RESEARCH CONSIDERABLY, allowing me long-distance access to archives in New Orleans. There I would contact Colleen Fitzpatrick, a most amazing genealogy fan who tracked her own New Orleans family in her spare time. I would learn she was indeed a "rocket scientist" with her own engineering firm in Orange County. Her mastery of five languages had resulted in her name appearing often in the growing databases of New Orleans records that had originally been written in French. Her knowledge of the language and the city where she grew up would prove invaluable. Her family name began with *F*, so it was easy for her to check the adjoining *E* names whenever she was posting information from birth and death indexes. Results from the New Orleans business directories stated who lived where, when, and what they did for a living. These would become vital to my reconstructing the family's various residences and business locations.

As these online archives grew, I was able to go back further and further to discover the early references spelled "Enard," without the *S*. In one archive there appeared to be a probate record for Etienne Enard in 1822, my earliest date so far. Colleen, the angel of genealogists, was heading south to check her own family information in the archives, which she knew better than anyone on earth. Generously, she offered to check into the probate office to see what was there.

A month later I received an email. "I hit a gold mine," she wrote. "What's your physical address? I'm sending you treasure."

I waited and in time a huge envelope arrived containing the complete probate inventory for Etienne's store on Burgundy Street. Every bit of fabric was recorded, every roll of ribbon, every tack, every piece of furniture, and various personal possessions. But this was not the real treasure.

Colleen had found the original affidavits from Nance, France, verifying Etienne's parents and siblings so that all would receive their share of the proceeds of the sale of the store. All of this apparently had been requested by the probate court before Pierre Charles Enard could be designated as executor to Etienne's estate. Oddly enough, in this same file was a later document upon Pierre Charles's death and probate. All he had left was an armoire and a few personal items. Clearly this man had not been as industrious as Etienne.

In Pierre Charles Esnard's probate record, Simeon Esnard is designated the beneficiary. It is unclear whether Simeon was the son of Etienne or Pierre Charles, as this has never been verified by birth records, but his death certificate states Simeon was colored. Since there was no census data stating Pierre Charles had ever cohabitated with a woman and Etienne was linked to Marie Felix for many years but could not marry legally, it is possible Simeon was their illegitimate son.

Colleen proved vital to reconstructing these early nineteenth-century records, both those public and online, and her personal service to me was invaluable. She continues to delve into genealogy and has become a professional researcher. I am forever in debt to her.

HELENE LEBERT

WIFE OF ANDRE LEBERT

Sur Seine, France, 1998

A MONG THE FAMILY PAPERS KEPT BY ANDRE LEBERT IN Paris were a series of letters sent between Florentine Krach Esnard and her sister in France, Pauline Krach Biche, that would span the years of the Great Migration from 1892 to 1930. After Josephine's death, Florentine Esnard and Jean Benjamin Esnard continued with more letters in this group. Virtually all were in French, so Helene carefully read and synopsized this massive amount of correspondence that dealt largely with the period after the 1888 *Dejan v. Dejan* trial and the challenges of Jim Crow legislation.

Helene did not translate the letters but took the information and wrote out the family saga with as many names, dates, and places, such as where Josephine was born, the death of Paul Krach, and how the French branch of the family reacted to their various changes over time. The letters are particularly valuable in detailing when and why the Esnards left New Orleans and the sometimes-fractious relationship between Florentine and her mother, Mama Dejan.

DIANA WILLIAMS

STUDENT

Harvard University, 1993

F ROM OCCASIONAL POSTINGS IN LOUISIANA GENEAL-
ogy sites about the Esnards, I received a phone call out of the blue one
day from Diana Williams, a student at Harvard researching her disser-
tation. It would be "They Call It Marriage," and she was focusing on the problems of interracial marriage in the South and how it was dealt with by the
free colored class. From her I would learn the first news that Jean Benjamin
was deeply involved in Reconstruction politics. She would also tell me about
Dejan v. Dejan and how well it revealed the entire family and its business
dealings at the time. "They're all in there testifying," she said. "And you can
find out how Jean Benjamin voted on racial matters in the archives as well."

Diana's contribution has been vital to learning the civil rights role of this
family and why the rise of Jim Crow was so threatening to their stability. It
would also reveal how *Dejan v. Dejan* made it impossible for the Esnards to
keep the family ancestry secret any longer.

❧

FLORENCE JUMONVILLE, PhD

LIBRARIAN

Earl K. Long Library, University of New Orleans

I T TOOK QUITE A WHILE FOR ME TO RUN DOWN THIS MYS-
terious Louisiana succession case, which I hoped held information I could
use to fill in the many gaps in the family story. But while in an airport
returning from New York, I realized that the case might be totally lost as
Hurricane Katrina rolled through New Orleans. The archives were at the
Earl K. Long Library on the campus of University of New Orleans, located
along the shore of Lake Ponchartrain. It was underwater. The likelihood that
any of the archives would survive was uncertain.

I would wait and watch as the people suffered before me on TV with the
federal government unable to help. Like so many Americans, I was appalled
at our inability to render aid to our own citizens. I emailed Colleen Fitzpatrick, who was naturally devastated by the loss of her beloved city, and as
reports came in of damaged city archives, I was so thankful she got the 1822
probate record out when she did.

I had been in contact with the library just before the hurricane, and they
had verified the case was there, but there was no time to copy it before the
flooding. So after the waters receded, I often called the library checking to
see if the phones were operational and whether anyone had returned . . . or
ever would. There was no way to know the extent of the damage, for in that
humid climate, even places that did not go underwater as the city library had
would be destroyed by damp and mold from being long closed and without
air-conditioning.

In the meantime, I researched the library online and found a picture of
the beautiful librarian, Miss Florence Jumonville, PhD. She posed for her
photograph in black velvet, a small dog on her lap. She would become my

160

fairy godmother of sorts, her actions proving her the epitome of an intellectual steel magnolia. Finally I reached her on the phone and sheepishly inquired about the copy of the court case. I was embarrassed to ask about something so insignificant in the wake of such an enormous human disaster. But dedicated as she was, Florence proved remarkably generous and verified that the archive I wanted was indeed protected. Her problem for the time being was that the copy machines were damaged by moisture, the toner fused. They had to be serviced. I immediately sent her a check for the library's page copy rate and waited.

I would receive an email from Florence a few weeks later saying the copy was made, but there was no reliable postal service in the city. She then took it upon herself to box up my order and drive it personally out of the city to a suburban post office where it was mailed.

Thanks to this woman's great effort and dedication to her state's history, I received over four hundred pages of *Dejan v. Dejan*. It was as Diana had said: the people I had been researching all along suddenly had a voice as the attorneys questioned them one after another in court. Suddenly it all came together and every one of them came alive again. This trial proved what the Dejan brothers had done to them all by forcing them to choose between racial anonymity or losing half their hard-earned fortune.

⚜

EPILOGUE

I FEEL PRIVILEGED TO BE THE ONE WHO HAS UNCOVERED the history of a family that embodies the struggles of the free colored class in New Orleans. Their unusual lives and their final move to Los Angeles is a tale that deserves to be told. There will be some who do not like what is in these pages, for even today they do not want these secrets revealed. But once I began my journey down this road, it felt as though a dozen voices urged me on, their whispers driving me to search deeper and deeper until all the details were uncovered.

I too have paid a price for bringing the Esnard-Dejan family back to life. My father is devastated that he is linked to African ancestry and that those he knew never shared this secret with him. He is so offended, he is in denial about it all, insisting the research is

This iconic photograph taken before Adrien's visit to Los Angeles may have been taken in the Raymond Street back-yard. It shows Jean Benjamin just before his death, right arm behind him hiding his smoking cigar. On the far right is his son, Paul Filbert, the jeweler. Between them is Paul Filbert's son, Raoul Esnard, MD, and in front on the leopard is Little Paul, the author's father. The leopard was sent by Adrien to the family, and it would be handed down to Little Paul and was well known among his children.

erroneous, and he will not discuss nor recognize it. My mother is equally uneasy with the discoveries. My brother has requested I not write the story. But these are just the California reactions.

Those in Baton Rouge and New Orleans still live in a world where color does matter. They have jumped the fence and don't want to go back. It is all because descendants of those Southern Democrats who drove the family out of New Orleans and fought the Civil Rights Movement are still hard at work driving away any of those with colored ancestry from their businesses, clubs, and social enclaves.

So here they are, from the first immigrant to the present day, written for our children. My twenty years of work and their lives dealing with racial struggle will not disappear again. All these people, white and colored, are our ancestors and now have a new voice so they may speak to us once again in triumph.

In many ways, the California Esnards were cut off from their southern ancestry. Such disassociation left the immediate offspring of those who relocated during the Great Migration equally as severed from their family histories as we were. It has always been my belief that children who grow up knowing their ancestors have a strong sense of who they are. Those predecessors who managed to overcome the challenges of immigration, poverty, and the right of marriage show new generations that they too can overcome their personal struggles.

A Catholic priest once explained to me that the saints are much like the players depicted on baseball cards. Children avidly collect them, pouring over favorite players and their individual statistics. Saints depicted on holy cards are much the same, that priest said. They are our favorite players, each offering us a reminder of their life story rife with sacrifice, triumph, and faith. Such is true with our ancestors. We avidly collect information about them to remind us of their legacy.

This book is one that brings the faces and stories of our ancestors into a twenty-first-century conversation. The children of my generation have no link to their past after my father, Little Paul, passed way in 2012 at eighty-seven. My hope is that this book will serve as his memory, and as a reference for the youngsters of all the Esnards who fanned out across America. This is their own story with its favorite players of the nineteenth century. But it will also provide insight to the millions of other "colored" children in America who inhabit this nebulous racial category caught in a social limbo between the African-American world and the white one.

ABOUT THE AUTHOR

AUREEN ESNARD GILMER LOVES A MYSTERY. THE DAY she decided to find out about the old missionary in a family photo began a twenty-year treasure hunt for the reasons he ended up in the Belgian Congo a hundred years ago. Already an established author of eighteen books and a nationally syndicated columnist, her desire to find the answers required she trace all the Esnards of New Orleans back to the free people of color community unique to that ancient American city. "It's as though they all spoke to me through the data, and helped me understand why there were so many secrets. I knew they wanted it to be written so that future generations would understand why they made certain very painful choices." The revelations would threaten Maureen's immediate family, but undaunted as always, she continued with the research that would bring ancestors out of the shadows and into the twenty-first century, inspiring future generations to stand up for their rights, beliefs, and faith. Maureen lives outside Palm Springs in the California high desert with her husband, Jim, two horses, and a pair of rescued pit bulls. Learn more about Maureen at MoPlants.com.